WRITERS AND CRITICS

Chief Editor
A. NORMAN JEFFARES

Advisory Editors
DAVID DAICHES
C. P. SNOW

With the publication of *Herzog*, Saul Bellow has established himself as the most important of the post-war American novelists. In his novels he has shown an increasingly profound understanding of the dilemmas and vexations of the alienated intelligent man in his modern urban *milieu*, explored the complex problems of self and community, and insisted on the need to move beyond the mood of alienation and discover more fruitful attitudes.

Tony Tanner's book is the first to be written on Bellow. It offers a close critical reading of each novel and also quotes generously from many important essays and stories by Bellow which are not easily obtainable. In addition it relates Bellow to the relevant literary traditions—Jewish, Russian, and American. Mr Tanner teaches at Cambridge where he is a Fellow of King's College. He has spent three years doing research in America and is the author of a long study of American literature called *The Reign of Wonder* (C.U.P. 1965). He has also written numerous articles on nineteenth- and twentieth-century English and American literature.

B—A

SAUL BELLOW

TONY TANNER

NEW   YORK

BARNES & NOBLE, INC.

Publishers · Booksellers . Since 1873

OLIVER AND BOYD LTD
Tweeddale Court
Edinburgh 1

39A Welbeck Street
London, W.1

Published in the United States
in 1965
by Barnes & Noble Inc.
New York, N.Y.

First published 1965

© 1965 Text and Bibliography
Tony Tanner

Printed in Great Britain by
Oliver and Boyd Ltd, Edinburgh

CONTENTS

ACKNOWLEDGMENTS

First I would like to thank Saul and Susy Bellow for the kindness and hospitality they extended to me in America. (This should not be taken to imply that Mr Bellow has given his approval to any of the comments on his work offered in this book.) Secondly I would like to express my gratitude to Professor Edward Shils who read this book in manuscript. Edward Shils's fluent and informed intelligence will be well known to those who have come in touch with him, and I have profited from his observations and ideas. Thirdly I would like to express my gratitude to Pascal Covici of the Viking Press for his co-operation. Lastly I want to acknowledge a personal debt to Marcia Albright for her help, interest, and sympathy during the writing of this book. My gratitude is only imperfectly expressed by the dedication.

For permission to quote from Saul Bellow's works, acknowledgments are due to Saul Bellow, Encyclopaedia Britannica Ltd., *Encounter*, the Macmillan Company, *New Leader*, *The Reporter*, *Saturday Review*, the *Times Literary Supplement*, Vanguard Press, Viking Press, and Weidenfeld & Nicolson Ltd.

The picture on the front cover is reproduced by permission of Jeff Lowenthal.

T. T.

To
MARCIA

ABBREVIATED TITLES
BY WHICH BELLOW'S WORKS
ARE CITED IN REFERENCES

Page references are identical in both English and American editions, unless otherwise stated.

A.M.	=	*The Adventures of Augie March.*
D.M.	=	*Dangling Man.*
H.	=	*Herzog.*
H.R.K.	=	*Henderson the Rain King.*
S.T.D.	=	*Seize the Day.*
T.V.	=	*The Victim.*

CHAPTER I

AN OUT AND OUT CHICAGOAN

. . . there is yet, to whoever is eligible among us, the prophetic vision, the joy of being toss'd in the brave turmoil of these times.—Walt Whitman.

Concerning the details of his personal life let Saul Bellow speak for himself.

My parents emigrated to Canada from Russia in 1913—my father, a business man, has often told me that he imported Egyptian onions into St. Petersburg —and settled in the town of Lachine, Quebec. I was born there in 1915, the youngest of four children. Until I was nine years old we lived in one of the poorest and most ancient districts of Montreal, on the Slope of St. Dominick Street between the general hospital and Rachel Market. In 1924 we moved to Chicago. I grew up there and consider myself a Chicagoan, out and out. Educated after a fashion in the Chicago schools, I entered the University of Chicago in 1933. . . . In 1935 I transferred to Northwestern University. . . . My intelligence revived somewhat and I graduated with honors in anthropology and sociology in 1937. Graduate school didn't suit me, however. I had a scholarship at the University of Wisconsin, and I behaved very badly. During the Christmas vacation, having fallen in love, I got married and never returned to the University. In my innocence, I had decided to become a writer.[1]

In fact his departure from University life was by no means final. For intermittent peroids Bellow has lived by free-lance writing, but for the most part he has

combined the profession of writer with that of teacher
considering, rightly enough, that it is better for a writer
to be a responsible educator than a hack-journalist
or a desperate Bohemian. He has taught at the University of Minnesota, Princeton, New York University,
Bard College, and—currently—the University of
Chicago. During the War he was for a time in the
Merchant Marine. His anthropological studies took him
to Mexico (but never to Africa) and in 1955 he spent
some time on an Indian reservation in Nevada where
he wrote *Seize the Day*. He has spent some time in
Europe, the longest trip being from 1948-50 during
which time he wrote much of *Augie March*. But most
of his life as a writer has been spent in New York,
Minnesota, or Chicago, and for the most part that
life has been related to University teaching.

Bellow's life has thus far been a very representative
American life: a life still intimately in touch with
immigrant experience, a life deeply immersed in the
vast urban complexes of modern America, a life in
which position and identity have continually to be
discovered and defined, never inherited and assumed.
That his life has been so representative doubtless
contributes to the centrality and relevance his writing
has to-day. But the qualities and preoccupations of
his work are not simply the reflexions of a contemporary
mood. The strength of his work represents a coalescence
of energies, a convergence of traditions—Russian,
Jewish, American—which I shall endeavour to outline
in this chapter.

But first it is worth stressing that although Bellow is
very responsive to the immense flexibility and openness
of American life, he is a pertinent critic of some of the
dangers inherent in his own society.

. . . we Americans are in the grip of a boundless desire.
. . . That our desires are infinite does not mean that

we are spiritual; it only means that we are not sure
what satisfaction is.[2]

In a book review he offered some ruthless criticisms
of the "vacuity and mindlessness" of many prosperous
Americans:

> Love, duty, principle, thought, significance, everything
> is being sucked into a fatty and nerveless state of
> "wellbeing." My mother used to say of people who
> had had a lucky break, in the old Yiddish metaphor,
> "they've fallen into the schmaltz-grub"—a pit of fat.
> The pit has expanded now into a swamp, and the
> lucky ones may be those who haven't yet tasted the
> fruits of prosperity.[3]

He took up the point from a different angle when he
reviewed Oscar Lewis's book on Mexico called *Five
Families*. In particular he discusses the new middle-class
family, the Castros:

> The lives of the Castros with their new wealth stand
> as a warning that the heart may empty as the belly
> fills. . . . Human history can fairly be described upon
> one level as the history of scarcity, and now that
> technology extends the promise of an increase of
> wealth we had better be aware of a poverty of the
> soul as terrible as that of the body. The lives of the
> poor move us, awaken compassion, but improvement
> of their lot merely by the increase of goods and
> comforts deprives them of the sense of reality based
> upon their experience of scarcity.[4]

Bellow returned to this point at great length in an
essay written after a trip through the boring, mechan-
ised, gaudy suburbia in Illinois. "Some important
ingredients of life were conspicuously absent." He asked
people what they did that was worth writing about—and
the answer was that there was nothing worth writing
about in their lives.

Was the vitality of these people entirely absorbed by the new things? Had a superior inventive and productive power taken them over, paralyzing all the faculties it did not need? Or had the old understanding of reality been based on the threat of hunger and on the continual necessity for hard labor?

But he notes that good books are still taken out of the library and he wonders what a woman does with privately acquired intelligence and cultivation and ideas. "They would be her discovery, her treasure ten times sealed, her private source of power." Then he extends the question: what do they, what do we, make of great works now that we are surrounded by T.V. and Hollywood, etc.

Our understanding of them (it is time to drop the third person) will certainly be faulty. Nevertheless, they move us. That is to say, human greatness can still be seen by us. And it is not a question of the gnat who sees the elephant. We are members not of a different species. Without a certain innate sympathy we could not read Shakespeare and Cervantes. In our own contemporary novels this power to understand the greatest human qualities appears to be dispersed, transformed or altogether buried. A modern mass society has no open place for such qualities, no vocabulary for them and no ceremony (except in churches) which makes them public. So they remain private and are mingled with other private things which vex us or of which we feel ashamed. But they are not lost. The saleswoman in Moline, Ill., *will* go to the library and borrow *Anna Karenina*. This society with its titanic products conditions but cannot absolutely denature us. It forces certain elements of the genius of our species to go into hiding. In America they take curiously personal, secret forms. Sometimes

> they corrupt people; sometimes they cause them to
> act with startling generosity. On the whole they
> are not to be found in what we call our Culture.
>
> They are not in the streets, in the stores, at the
> movies. They are the missing ingredients.[6]

Thus Bellow admits that society with its increasing
materialism threatens to suffocate the soul with its
profusion of things. But, he asserts, the human spirit
is inextinguishable. Society may move towards its
death with false concepts of progress and prosperity—
but somewhere, somehow, the human spirit will start
to disengage itself, to protest, to assert its need for true
values, for real freedom, for genuine reality. Now this
sense of the abiding human spirit as an essence in its own
right which can take issue with a whole society, a whole
state of affairs, we may fairly call Russian. The European
novel rarely envisages so naked a confrontation. There
society is felt to be the inexorable arena in which life
is worked out: destiny is social destiny, people find—or
lose—their reality somewhere within the established
amenities and restrictions of complex community life.
In the great Russian novel, society, even when brilliantly
described and realised, is seldom felt to be the ultimate
condition and container of man. So often there is
the sense of extreme human needs, compulsions, forces
which can dissolve, dismiss or transcend the social
limits of life. There the human spirit is a tremendous
palpable reality capable of scattering and distancing
any claims that the material world is the ultimate
reality. And it is surely not for nothing that Bellow
often refers to the great Russians:

> Like it or not, says Dostoyevsky, it is our nature to be
> free, and under the sting of suffering to choose between
> good and evil. And Tolstoy says of human nature

that it contains a need for truth which will never allow it to rest permanently in falsehood or unreality.[7]

I am suggesting that Bellow drew nourishment and vigour from the great Russian writers, and particularly because they often assert, with irresistible conviction, the ability of the human spirit to deny and invalidate a whole range of false social values and reaffirm the priceless freedom, independence, and integrity of the self. Most importantly, it was the Russian writers who most vividly questioned and opposed the nineteenth-century European ideals of materialistic pleasure and comfort as the measure of human progress. Tolstoy increasingly came to feel that the dominating concept of infinite progress would gradually drain all the meaning and significance out of the finite life of man; his own biography graphically demonstrates the measure of his disillusion with society.[8] And Dostoevsky produced the most scathing denial of the complacent notion of enlightened self-interest and utilitarian progress towards a materialistic Utopia written during the whole century.[9] Bellow admits to the influence of Dostoevsky in his early work and some of the gestures and arguments of his characters do recall that figure who refused so memorably to accept the progress of society, who stood out against the strong drift of material happiness in order to assert the independence of the human spirit: "one's own free, unrestrained choice, one's own whim, be it the wildest, one's own fancy, sometime worked up to a frenzy." This, of course, is the narrator of *Notes from Underground* who from the squalid pit of his renunciation makes one very disturbing assertion:

So I may still turn out to be more *alive* than you in the end. Come on, have a look at it! Why, today we don't even know where real life is, what it is, or what it's called! Left alone without literature, we immediately become entangled and lost—we don't know what to join, what to keep up with; what to love, what to hate; what to respect; what to despise! We even find it painful to be men—real men of flesh and blood, with *our own private bodies*; we're ashamed of it, and we long to turn ourselves into something hypothetical called the average man. We're stillborn . . . and we like it better and better.[10]

Contemporary American society has often provoked Bellow into making similar indictments. Many of his characters, too, refuse society's values and dislodge themselves from its drift in order to celebrate the independence and freedom of the self alive.

But Bellow's important characters do not stay underground, and Dostoevsky's profound and lacerating metaphysical ironies are replaced by a move towards something more euphoric and affirmative. This brings me to the second influence on Bellow's work—Jewish writing. With no knowledge of Yiddish it would be impertinent of me to suggest how much Bellow owes to his knowledge of the language and its literature. I shall therefore quote at length from a revealing review he wrote of Sholom Aleichem's *The Adventures of Motel the Cantor's Son*.

The Jews of the ghetto found themselves involved in an immense joke. They were divinely designated to be great and yet they were like mice. History was something that *happened* to them; they did not make it. The nations made it, while they, the Jews, suffered it. But when history had happened it belonged to them, inasmuch as it was the coming of the Messiah— *their* Messiah—that would give it meaning. Every male child was potentially the Messiah. The most ordinary Yiddish conversation is full of the grandest historical, mythological, and religious allusions. The Creation, the Fall, the Flood, Egypt, Alexander, Titus, Napoleon, the Rothschilds, the sages, and the Laws may get into the discussion of an egg, a clothes-line, or a pair of pants. This manner of living on terms of familiarity with all times and all greatness contributed, because of the poverty and powerlessness of the Chosen, to the ghetto's sense of the ridiculous. Powerlessness appears to force people to have recourse to words. Hamlet has to unpack his heart with words, he complains. The fact that the Jews of Eastern Europe lived among menacing and powerful neighbours no doubt contributed to the subtlety and richness of the words with which they unpacked.[11]

I need hardly emphasise the relevance of this to Bellow's own style in which the pants and the philosophy come bundled up together; indeed he elsewhere commends Montaigne's ability "to pass with ease from kitchen matters to metaphysics" adding that "this mixture of things high and low is peculiarly modern."[12] It also appears to be peculiarly Jewish and certainly contributes to the richness and humour of his own "unpacking" style.

Clearly some of the stock figures, as well as the style, of Jewish writing have influenced Bellow. For instance in writing of Aleichem's novel he points approvingly to the "boundless resilience" of the small boy in it. "Almost nothing can take place which he is unable to make into an occasion of happiness. . . . All places are alike to him. He declines to suffer the penalties the world imposes on him." Bellow invests some of his own characters with such a resilience. And of course those traditional Jewish figures the *schnorrer* and *schlemiel*, the fall-guy, the innocent fool, are part of the furniture of Bellow's imagination. It is worth noting that Bellow translated "Gimpel the Fool" by Isaac Bashevis Singer. Gimpel is a fool in his tolerance and good nature and credulity. He endures everything a malicious world can put on him, with good humour. "Shoulders are from God, and burdens too." He finds that the whole world deceives him, but after a momentary lapse into cynicism he goes out to wander in the world, listening to everything until he comes to the conclusion "that there were really no lies." He accepts everything and is supremely wise in his folly: "no doubt the world is entirely an imaginary world, but it is only once removed from the true world."[13] Again we shall find Bellow drawn to such fools who persist in their folly, thereby becoming, as Blake promised, wise.

Leslie Fiedler tends to believe that in the post-war period of atomisation, uprooting, and "universal alien-ation" the "image of the Jew tends to become the image of everyone."[14] One thing is certainly true, namely that in America to-day the most important and central fiction is being written by Jewish writers. Ever since Abraham Cahan's novel *The Rise of David Levinsky* (1917) there has been an increasing number of works about Jewish urban experience, works of varying quality by people like Ludwig Lewisohn, Waldo Frank, Ben Hecht, Clifford Odets, as well as the more poetic and "absurd" analyses of American society offered by writers like Daniel Fuchs, Henry Roth, and Nathaneal West. Certainly, as Fiedler says, Bellow's work represents the full flowering of an existing tradition. (This is not the place to discuss this tradition in detail. Anyone interested would do well to read Isaac Rosenfeld's novel *Passage from Home*. Rosenfeld, a friend of Bellow's was a promising writer who died tragically young—Bellow paid tribute in an obituary[15] —and his novel is about a young boy growing up in a Jewish family in Chicago. It may well have influenced Bellow.)

B—B

But Bellow is not only in a tradition of Jewish-American writing; he is fairly in the major traditions of American literature which date from the nineteenth century. In particular his work relates him quite clearly to Whitman and Dreiser. In *Democratic Vistas*—pessimistic as to American facts, optimistic as to American possibilities—Whitman discusses a crucial paradox which is as much at the heart of Bellow's work as his own. Whitman voiced as nobody else did the American dream of a new society without rank, degree, or privilege, a new harmonious community based on love and equality, a new "ensemble" in which all people were to be merged democratically together. But he also celebrated an even more important principle—the free unencumbered self.

> For to democracy, the leveler, the unyielding principle of the average, surely join'd another principle, equally unyielding, closely tracing the first, indispensable to it, opposite. . . . This second principle is individuality, the pride and centripetal isolation of a human being in himself—identity—personalism.[16]

Whitman's song is ultimately of the self and not society; his theme is "the all-varied, all-permitting, all-free theorem of individuality." He was the first writer to be so clearly aware of a problem which was to occupy the American imagination for generations to come. As a recent critic has put it: "A common theme of the American imagination has been the problem of reconciling individual freedom with a mode of social life to which the individual can give his allegiance without danger of impairing his moral, spiritual, or psychological integrity."[17] Whitman's formulation of the problem deserves to stand prominently in the foreground of our discussion:

The problem, as it seems to me, presented to the New World, is, under permanent law and order, and after preserving cohesion (ensemble-Individuality), at all hazards, to vitalize man's free play of special Personalism, recognizing in it something that calls ever more to be consider'd, fed, and adopted as the substratum for the best that belongs to us (government indeed is for it), including the new aesthetics of the future.[18]

He stresses the supreme value of the "native personality," an intrinsic value not dependent on culture or knowledge or intellect. At the same time, he wants a new "ensemble," a valid community. Not only do all these ideas and problems recur in Bellow's work, the poet-narrator of *Song of Myself* seems like a forefather of many of Bellow's own narrators. Not only because of his rich vernacular which is almost greedily hospitable to kitchen matters and metaphysics alike, but also because of his actions and movements within the poem. I can make my point best by piecing together some quotations from Richard Chase's admirable book *Walt Whitman Reconsidered*:

. . . the "self" who is the protagonist of Whitman's poem is a character portrayed in a recognisable American way. It illustrates the fluid, unformed personality exulting alternatively in its provisional attempts to define itself and in its sense that it has no definition. . . . Of great importance is the fact that most of "Song of Myself" has to do not with the self searching for a final identity but with the self escaping a series of identities which threaten to dissolve its lively and various spontaneity. . . . The motif of "Song of Myself" is the self taking on a bewildering variety of identities and with a truly virtuous agility extracting itself from each one.[19]

With little change that could stand as a description of
Augie March. And just as that novel was originally
entitled *Among the Machiavellians* because of its theme
of society's concerted efforts to trap and arrest the wary,
resilient self, so Whitman's poem also deals with various
threats to individual freedom and identity. Chase
summarises: "The poet's 'identity' is said to be assailed
and warped into other 'identities' by agents referred
to as 'traitors', 'Wasters' and 'marauders'. Somewhat
elusive in particular, these appear to have in common
a quality of aggressiveness and imperiousness. They act
as a radical individualist conceives society to act.
They break down the self, they swagger, they assert
conviction, responsibility, and reason, they dominate
and impose passivity and furtiveness on the individual."
Yet with all his concern for individuality, Whitman
did believe in the idea of a good society but, paradoxi-
cally, one which would somehow emerge from individual
freedom. "As a moralist Whitman shares with Emerson
his belief that the self can be self-sufficient and that
merely by being good, free, various, spontaneous, and
loving enough, it can extrude, as it were, the good
society."[20] All of these convictions, aspirations, problems,
and dreams recur throughout Bellow's work.

Of course many other American writers have created
figures who dramatise the equivocal relationship
between the uncommitted self and society with its various
demands for commitment and capitulation: Huck
Finn, improvising his own destiny, refuses to be civilised
having been there once; Melville's Bartleby with his cry
which echoes forever through American literature—" I
would prefer not to," not to be reasonable, not to play
society's game any way it is offered, preferring the un-
approachable independence of his immense aloneness;
Henry James's American who has the "look of being
committed to nothing in particular, of standing in an

attitude of general hospitality to the chances of life."
There are many others: they are often joyful, generous
with their wonder, naïve in their ideal expectations and
absence of preconceived judgment; they are often
deeply sad, vulnerable to disillusion, and condemned to
that kind of loneliness which is the price extracted for
their special kind of freedom. Augie is a member of an
honourable and long-established American lineage.

Along with this passionate celebration of the self,
American writers have also shown a voracious appetite
for the teeming stuff around them. The habit of simply
naming long lists of things should not be dismissed as
mere cataloguing but seen for what it is—an awed
accumulation, a sort of devotional gathering-in, a
delighted revelling in the profuse evidence of an in-
credibly fecund creation. Whitman has this as well,
but for the modern urban setting the important man is
Dreiser. Bellow's own testimony is relevant here. He
notes that American urban life has become so ugly that
many American writers cannot "lift up" the facts around
them and, to compensate, concentrate on developing
a special language of art. "Dreiser had no need for this
use of language because of his greater lifting power."
His painfully acquired knowledge of life at its toughest
and lowest "carried fairly easily facts that were too great
a burden to other writers."[21] One has only to read
Dreiser's account of Sister Carrie's first experience of
Chicago to get the idea of what Bellow well calls his
"lifting power." He grasps at the city in immense
handfuls, his objectivity not interrupted by aesthetic
wincings or moralising condemnations. And there is
more in Dreiser that appeals to Bellow. Consider Sister
Carrie. She is not a bad person, she has no guile or
rapacity, nor is she a saint. Her most urgent and
persistent motive is an unidentifiable yearning. "She
longed and longed and longed." But for what? She

still has not discovered at the end of the book, surrounded by material success. The teeming American city in which everything is in motion, unstable, transitory, continually shifting in value, is like a great sea. Some are dragged down to the very depths, like Hurstwood; others, through a combination of inner promptings and the solicitations and compulsions of circumstance are tossed to success, like Carrie herself. This is the modern American world; far denser, thicker, more impinging and engulfing than the world inhabited by Whitman's poet-narrator. What of the pure freedom of the self in this world; is it possible to preserve that old uncommitted independence of spirit in modern Chicago? Or is this sort of life, as Dreiser more than half felt, governed by " forces wholly superhuman." What indeed becomes of your vision of the unique value of the individual when life seems to be dominated by a freakish, heavy-handed determinism? Pessimism might seem to be the answer, and yet that is not the American way. Even Dreiser's fatalism cannot bring itself to turn a cold shoulder on life. As Bellow felt: "This is what is so moving in him, his balkiness and sullenness and then his allegiance to life. The fact that he is a modern Amercian gives an extreme edge to this allegiance; it is made after immersion in the greatest difficulties and reasons for pessimism and with all the art of which he is capable, and stubbornly insisted upon under the severest discouragements."[22] It is the not-spurning of anything or anyone that is Dreiser's great merit: to lift so much is in itself an affirmative gesture no matter how bleakly he feels about the impersonal forces bearing down on man.

Bellow, too, has to confront the problem of doing justice both to the claims of the individual will and the undoubted pressures of the immense urban complexes. If he has taken up Whitman's almost metaphysical joy

in the unrestrainable delight of the free human spirit,
so also he has absorbed Dreiser's far-reaching and vastly
honest urban determinism. Augie March is a little
like Whitman's poet-narrator having to make his way
through Sister Carrie's world. Bellow, too, has that
lifting power which is indispensable to an American
writer if he is to do justice to the bewildering plenitude
of his world. But since, as we suggested earlier, he does
not want to get stuck in that world, his writing also
reveals what we may call a great rejecting energy. He
can throw aside what he picks up. He neither capitulates
to the contemporary world nor does he renounce it.
The adventure all takes place between those too rigid,
extreme reactions. Aware of all that is corrupt and
destructive in the modern world, Bellow refuses to
traffic in pessimism. Refuses time after time, as we shall
see. What he says of Joyce Cary's writing applies to
his own:

> it accepts the contemporary, it defends the possibil-
> ities of the man of the present, denies that it is so very
> bad to be what we are or that we are born to be
> condemned with the times. It asserts that there are
> powerful and original natures to be found still, that
> genius exists, that striving is not necessarily mono-
> mania, happiness not extinct, hope not unjustified.
> "The marvel is that millions deny all hope and boast
> themselves wise," Mr. Cary's Nimmo earnestly says
> in *Except the Lord*.[23]

Not a fatuous optimism, but a "tenaciousness against
death"[24] is what Bellow asks from the novel writer,
and this tenaciousness his own work amply exhibits.
It opens itself fully to "the brave turmoil of these times".
It omits nothing. But it refuses to give up the possibility
of some "prophetic vision" to be gained, perhaps, at
the very heart of the here and now.

REFERENCES

1. *Twentieth Century Authors*, First Supplement, ed. Stanley Kunitz, 1955, pp. 72-3.

2. From the Foreword to *Winter Notes on Summer Impressions*, 1955.

3. "The Swamp of Prosperity," 1959.

4. "The Uses of Adversity," 1959.

5. "The Sealed Treasure," 1960.

6. *Op. cit.*

7. *Op. cit.*

8. See Max Weber's essay "Science as a Vocation," in *From Max Weber*, edd. Gerth and Wright Mills, 1958, pp. 139-40.

9. See Lionel Trilling's essay "The Fate of Pleasure" in *Romanticism Reconsidered*, ed. Northrop Frye, 1963.

10. All Dostoevsky quotations are from Andrew MacAndrew's translation in the Signet Classic ed.

11. "Laughter in the Ghetto," *Saturday Review of Literature*, 30 May, 1953. See also the introduction to *Great Jewish Short Stories*, ed. Saul Bellow, 1963.

12. *The Great Ideas Today*, 1963, p. 135.

13. *Partisan Review*, May-Jun. 1953.

14. "What can we do about Fagin?" in *Commentary*, May 1949. See also Saul Bellow, "The Jewish Writer and the English Literary Tradition," *Commentary*, Oct. 1949.

15. In *Partisan Review*, Fall 1956.

16. *Leaves of Grass and Selected Prose*, 1955 edn., p. 514.

17. A. N. Kaul, *The American Vision*, 1963, p. 14.

18. *Leaves of Grass and Selected Prose*, p. 518.

19. Richard Chase, *Walt Whitman Reconsidered*, 1955, pp. 60, 61, 65, 66.

20. *Op. cit.*, pp. 68, 69, 88.

21. "Dreiser and the Triumph of Art," 1951.

22. *Op. cit.*

23. Review of Joyce Cary, *A Personal Record*, in *New Republic* 22 Feb. 1954.

24. Review of Italian fiction, "Without Hope," in *New Leader*, 11 Dec. 1950.

CHAPTER II

THE CRATERS OF THE SPIRIT

Who can be the earnest huntsman of himself when
he is in turn a quarry? Or nothing so distinctive as
quarry, but one of a shoal, driven toward the weirs.
But I must know what I myself am.[1]

Bellow's first piece of published fiction appeared in 1941
and was entitled "Two Morning Monologues." (It was
a prophetic title, for much of Bellow's subsequent
work was to be based on a series of impressive monologists.) Not an ambitious work it nevertheless shows
him sounding out certain problems and themes which
are to recur and deepen in various forms throughout
his work. The two juxtaposed monologists are an
unemployed man waiting to be called up, and a small-
time gambler. The two types have a special interest
for Bellow. Both are alienated from the accepted values
and normal domestic-commercial routines which
surround them. Neither can accept what the world
seems to want to force on them, make of them.[2]

Two types, then: one nearly "sunk," the other mainly
a loser, both unwilling to participate in the accredited
routines of contemporary society. They both refuse to
be attached to their environment in any way. But one
is a passive resister, the other a pushing manipulator:
one is immobile, suspended, the other slips through,
finds a way round. Both are technically unemployed,
but one gambles while the other lounges: both preserve
their individuality, one by asocial assertion, the other
by asocial negation. The unemployed man is "driven"

but refuses to comply with the forceful drift; the gambler
sees all life as chance and accepts it, trying to twist it
to his own ends. The latter is a dodging, weaving,
risking man: the former is a withdrawing, denying,
dangling man. This analysis might seem disproportion-
ate to a slight short story, but the two types recur in
varying combinations and confrontations in the later
work. They serve to define one of Bellow's major areas
of inquiry ; namely, how should a man live, how can he
evade the stifling shape which society seeks to impose
on him, how preserve the freedom to be himself in
a world which seems to offer only intolerable
alternatives?

Dangling Man was published in 1944 and consists of
the diary entries of an unemployed man awaiting his
call-up. These entries cover the four months prior to
his decision to volunteer and they focus on the sequence
of incidents, meditations, and moods which precede
and precipitate that equivocal decision. In many ways
Joseph, the diarist, seems to exist in a permanently
benumbed state, out of reach of the world and not
fully moored in it. The American hero has, indeed,
habitually been thrown back upon himself, enduring
a state of sombre aloneness which survives all surface
changes of mood. No matter what relish of life he
evinces, he often gives the air of brooding apart, though
the apartness is not a state of supine self-pity. Usually
he is questing, searching, speculating, either for some
superior form of truth, or some richer reality, or some
affirmative mode of true reconciliation with the world
he inclines to renounce. But Joseph's America has
fallen under the shadow of Hitler's Europe and instead
of Thoreau's pastoral self-communing, his diary aches
with the exacerbated self-probing of a man up to his
neck in modern history. Joseph oscillates between
corrosive inertia and compulsive self-inquiry, wrestling

with irresolvable paradoxes of world and spirit which
have a drastically deleterious effect on his character
and bring him to the point of futility and exhaustion.

From the first page the journal reveals a man
approaching complete demoralisation. He rarely leaves
the room and is often alone all day. Books no longer
hold his attention and he seems almost completely
indifferent to his wife. A "narcotic dullness" has gripped
him, though he does have moments of "bewilderment
and vexation" in which he sees himself as a "moral
casualty of the war." The faster the outer world seems
to move, the more "stock-still" does he become until
he feels "rooted to my chair." "Bitterness and spite"
are eating away at his "endowment of generosity and
good will." From one point of view he is involved
in a trivial "bureaucratic comedy": having resigned
his job to answer the army's call for induction he simply
has to wait until he is drafted. He could hasten the
process by volunteering or he could get another job:
"but I am unwilling to admit that I do not know how
to use my freedom and have to embrace the flunkydom
of a job because I have no resources—in a word, no
character."[3] But his "freedom" from any sort of involvement and *rapprochement* with the world has turned him
into a "dangling man," devoid of all positive impulses
and constructive initiative. His freedom is a void in
which he hangs, unable to reach any solid reality.
His journal is not a mere hobby but a strategy to retain
his sanity. The insensitive can satisfy themselves with
physical action; Joseph because of his candour and
habit of introspection has only one last resource—"to
talk to myself." The dialogue of civilisation has broken
down. The very persistence with which Bellow follows
the movements of this doomed awareness as it eats away
at itself prompted Edmund Wilson to say of the book:
it is "one of the most honest pieces of testimony on the

psychology of a whole generation who have grown up
during the war."⁴

This book is not totally sealed off, for Joseph does
make occasional forays into the outside world. But
these forays usually end in a mess or a row, ironically
serving to throw Joseph deeper into himself. He wanders
among: he is not related to. And this pattern—of
attempted insertion into the world and disgusted withdrawal from it—is the external shape of his internal
problem. And if at times he seems lazy and indifferent,
merely passive and drained of all human feeling to the
point of dead neutrality, we should be aware of the
immense frustration and anguish that these apparent
failings conceal. "Lazy we are not. When we seem so,
our cyclonic wishes are baffled, and pride requires us
to be indifferent."⁵ In later works Bellow is to release
those "cyclonic wishes": but here he is trying to understand and describe their bewilderment, their baffled
arrest. For although Joseph keeps a "tight hold" on
his self and inner being, resisting all "encumbrances,"
he also has another yearning—for true society. He was
a "creature of plans": he wanted "'a colony of the spirit'
or a group whose covenants forbade spite, bloodiness,
and cruelty."⁶ Once he thought he had the material
for this community of the elect, but a squalid party
brings home to him the fatal weaknesses and bitter
shortcomings of his friends. Inside and outside oneself
"there were so many treasons" which rendered the ideal
impossible of realisation. But his yearning remains.
"The plan could be despised; my need could not be."⁷
Disillusion thrusts him back into himself where at least he
can cherish a sense of individual value and importance.
But "goodness is achieved not in a vacuum, but in the
company of other men, attended by love. I, in this
room, separate, alienated, distrustful, find in my purpose
not an open world, but a closed, hopeless jail. My

perspectives end in the walls."[8] Emerging with the
hunger to establish an ideal community of love, Joseph
finds himself in a squalid jungle where selfishness,
rapacity, and spite range at large: withdrawing to
preserve the integrity of the self, he finds himself in a
prison which damages his sense of reality and devalues
his life through stagnation. In spending himself he
wasted himself; saving himself he is now losing himself.
Jungle or prison. Or the War. Such is his problem;
such is his choice. Such is his "freedom."

This is a key word in the book. Thus a late burst of
clarity:

> All the striving is for one end. I do not entirely
> understand this impulse. But it seems to me that
> its final end is the desire for pure freedom. We are
> all drawn toward the same craters of the spirit—to
> know what we are and what we are for, to know our
> purpose, to seek grace.[9]

Man must make the descent into the deep hollows of
his being in order to attain to that self-knowledge which
is the indispensable condition of purposive action and
the earning of grace. But "pure freedom"? Is this freedom
from something, or freedom to be or do something?
Another passage:

> We struggle perpetually to free ourselves. Or, to put
> it somewhat differently, while we seem so intently
> and even desperately to be holding on to ourselves,
> we would far rather give ourselves away. We do not
> know how. So, at times, we throw ourselves away.
> When what we really want is to stop living so exclus-
> ively and vainly for our own sake, impure and un-
> knowing, turning inward and self-fastened.[10]

This would be freedom from that ruinous self-
preoccupation which is a particular danger in a culture

which celebrates the unique value of the isolate individual; it would be the freedom which ensues when
one manages to find some "ideal construction" to help
one to "unlock the imprisoning self." The self must
be transcended, but to what end? Who or what is to
receive the gift of the dedicated and transcended self?
A man with a faith or an ideology could confidently
say, in Thy service is perfect freedom: but Joseph has
no God and no Party. He does not want to be "humped
protectively over my life" but he can find nothing
to which he can fruitfully dedicate it. Society stifles
rather than fulfills: yet a man rots on his own. He is
right to hold on to the self against society's coercive
and degrading influences; on the other hand "it is a
different thing to value oneself, and to prize oneself
crazily."[11] Does he over-value the self, is it mere pride
which makes him hold himself back as though expecting
"a separate destiny"? Intermittently he realises that
"a man must accept limits." He both wants and fears
to have limits set. Joseph is a very typical American
figure in this—that he would like some ideal to help to
give shape to his random life, yet he is distrustful of all
shaping forces; he would like to be committed to some
"exclusive focus" and yet he reveals an ineradicable
dislike for any commitments that life offers. Anxious
to be positive he nevertheless spends much of his life
negating.

The truth of the book is the firm grip Bellow has on
the paradox of unusable freedom. In his period of
waiting, Joseph is technically "free": no job holds him
down, the army has not yet summoned him to its
disciplined ranks. Yet he is driven to make this critical
confession to himself. "If I were a little less obstinate,
I would confess failure and say that I do not know what
to do with my freedom."[12] As Bellow has written "you
must manage your freedom or drown in it."[13] This book

follows a man trying and failing to "manage" his freedom. And the end is a kind of drowning. Joseph finally capitulates, since his ideals have turned rancid in the contemporary atmosphere and his own freedom has become merely a morose accidie. And in doing so he becomes a representative victim of the times. His final entries in the diary add up to a summary abandonment of the values he has tussled with throughout the book:

I am no longer to be held accountable for myself;
I am grateful for that. I am in other hands, relieved
of self-determination, freedom cancelled.
Hurray for regular hours!
And for the supervision of the spirit!
Long live regimentation![14]

This is not necessarily total cynicism, but it does represent a defeat. For what Joseph has to admit, reluctantly, to himself, is true. "I had not done well alone."[15]

Nevertheless there is a stubborn refusal to relapse into total pessimism. Perhaps this is most marked in Joseph's response to the city and its atmosphere. The city is, almost without exception, foul, mucky, sick, soiling, and soiled, and Joseph is piercingly aware of the dehumanising effect of all its squalid detritus: but he notes it all without the nausea of total rejection. Certainly he seems to be living in a "condemned age." But "how did we know it was? In all principal ways the human spirit must have been the same."[16] Joseph— and Bellow—maintain this as an article of faith, no matter how the evidence piles up to the contrary. The inclination is to repudiate, but "there might be a chance that I was misled, even with these ruins before my eyes."[17] The search for the eternal human spirit among the vast ruins of modern civilisation is the spur for more than one Bellow figure. This refusal of final condemnation and denial of the modern world emerges more clearly in a long interior dialogue. Projecting one half of himself into a presence he calls the "Spirit of Alternatives," he thrashes out the question of alienation. I will run together some key statements in the argument:

> There's a lot of talk about alienation. It's a fool's plea. . . . You can't banish the world by decree if it's in you. . . . The world comes after you. . . . Whatever you do, you cannot dismiss it. . . . . It's too easy to abjure it or detest it. Too narrow. Too cowardly. . . . The failing may be in us, in me. A weakness of vision.[18]

Admitting how little fond he is of the surrounding world, Joseph makes an important distinction. "I didn't say there was no feeling of alienation, but that we should not make a doctrine of our feeling."[19] In a word, alienation is felt but refused. Joseph is an intellectual, a solitary thinker; yet even he feels that true reality is somewhere out there in the muck and mire of the world, enduring and always to be found. Recalling his slum upbringing with all its cruelty and violence, he nevertheless feels it was "the only place where I was ever allowed to encounter reality."[20] Later Bellow protagonists are to hurl themselves far more forcefully into the seething ruck of the external world, to "sound creation through other means": but, like him, they will also be avid inquirers and thinkers, and, like him also, they will be wary of being trapped and immobilised. Thus a basic rhythm is set up even in this book by the most alienated of Bellow's characters. Approach and retreat; immersion and emancipation; involvement and disentanglement. The desire for community is counterbalanced by the instinct for flight: plunges into what William James called "the rich thicket of reality" are offset by lonely flights of metaphysics. It is in fact a classic American rhythm or pattern. It is Bellow's distinction to have applied it with such relevance to his age.

Bellow's first novel is in some ways crude. One occasionally has the feeling that problems, preoccupations, and scraps of random reading are tumbled onto the pages rather unrelatedly. Like disturbed birds, thoughts swarm up somewhat wildly from the scattering of recorded incidents. And the diary form as here used carries with it the danger of solipsism—a danger we shall note later in connexion with other work. Yet his themes are engaged with an involving seriousness. Bellow's choice of *genre* is dictated by the desperate quest his characters share—the need for "comprehension." As Joseph noted, freedom without comprehension is barely the beginning of freedom. Much of the action in Bellow's work is in the working of the inquiring mind: the push towards understanding is itself dramatic. And when we see later characters pull themselves up out of the craters of the spirit and get out into the world we should realise that their driving hunger is for knowledge—of themselves, of the world. Passive or active, involved or withdrawn, assertive or put-upon, they are all engaged in the supreme adventure of comprehension.

REFERENCES

1. *D.M.*, p. 119.
2. "Two Morning Monologues," 1941.
3. *D.M.*, p. 12.
4. *New Yorker*, 1 Apr. 1944.
5. *D.M.*, p. 133.
6. *D.M.*, p. 39.
7. *D.M.*, p. 57.
8. *D.M.*, p. 92.
9. *D.M.*, p. 154.
10. *D.M.*, pp. 153-4.

11. *D.M.*, p. 88.
12. *D.M.*, p. 151.
13. "The University as Villian," 1957.
14. *D.M.*, p. 191.
15. *D.M.*, p. 190.
16. *D.M.*, p. 25.
17. *Ibid.*
18. *D.M.*, p. 137.
19. *D.M.*, p. 138.
20. *D.M.*, p. 86.

B—C

CHAPTER III

A KIND OF RECOGNITION

Eyes seemed softer than by day, and larger, and
gazed at one longer, as though in the dark heat some
interspace of reserve had been crossed and strangers
might approach one another with a kind of recognition. You looked and thought, at least, that you
knew whom you had seen.[1]

In 1947 Bellow published his second novel, *The Victim*.
It was well received by the critics and Diana Trilling's
comment that it is "morally one of the farthest-reaching
books our contemporary culture has produced" is a
representative acclaim. In this novel Bellow is again
probing down into the problem of what the self owes
the self and what the self owes the rest of the world;
to what extent should a man permit himself to be
limited by the claims of other people; where does the
privilege of individuality run up against the responsibilities of inter-relatedness? For an introductory quota-
tion he draws on the tale from the *Arabian Nights* about
the merchant who threw away some date stones only
to find himself confronted by a huge Ifrit who says that
the date stones killed his son and who now claims
reparation and revenge. The moral is profound: slight
unintentional acts can have terrible consequences, we
never know whom we touch or how we wound. Some
of this was considered in Bellow's first novel, but here
the problems are engaged much more profoundly
because he has found a truly dramatic situation which
gradually exposes the problems instead of merely
discussing them in a series of unmoored speculations.

The surface story is simply told: Asa Leventhal, a middle-aged editor of a small trade magazine, is temporarily left alone in New York when his wife goes to visit her mother. Suddenly he is accosted by a remote acquaintance, Kirby Allbee, who is now little better than a bum. Allbee insists that Leventhal was responsible for his losing his job, and thus for his subsequent fall into the social depths. Leventhal denies the charge as fantastic, the lunatic accusation of an anti-Semite, and repudiates Allbee's claims for some sort of reparation. But Allbee persists in his pursuit of Leventhal and gradually Leventhal comes to acknowledge some guilt, some responsibility, and some relationship. "I haven't thought about you in years, frankly, and I don't know why you think I care whether you exist or not. What, are we related?" That is his first reaction to the importunate Allbee. And the latter's answer—"By blood? No, no. . . . heavens!"[2]—opens up the central theme of the book. How is man related to man—not brother to brother, or Jew to Jew, but men as seemingly remote as the anti-Semitic degenerate failure from an old New England family, and the wary, cautious, increasingly successful immigrant Jew. Dreiser clearly stands behind Bellow here, in this account of success and failure crossing each other in the seething motion and matter of the big city: but Dostoevsky is also there—particularly the Dostoevsky of tales like *The Double* with their accounts of the feverish and maddened psyche at large in inexplicable and apparently hostile *milieux*.

Asa Leventhal is ordinary enough to be a type of everyman. Happily married, moderately successful, not very responsive or attractive, but decent enough and content to mind his own business. But that is only the man-in-the-street surface. The few days which the novel concentrates on reveal the sluggishly stirring depths under the superficial ordinariness. It is perhaps significant that his wife is away: she, he acknowledges, is the power which maintains routine, "normalcy," the domestic order which is the strongest refuge against any troubling irregularity. The novel catches Leventhal exposed, vulnerable; and in this state other weaknesses, sicknesses even, erupt within and relentlessly start to shake him. He has to pass through illness and chaos to earn his wider awareness and fuller recognition of the human lot. The novel starts by showing him reluctantly answering a summons from his sister-in-law whose husband is away and whose baby is sick. Such traditional duty ordained by ties of blood he does not fail to perform, even if it is grudgingly. But also from the start of the novel a deep *malaise* seems to have fallen on him. His external appearance, "unaccommodating, impassive,"[3] is racked and undermined and troubled by physical sickness, exacerbated by hypochondria, sudden upwelling feelings of guilt, and a devouring, warping paranoia. He is "disappointed and dissatisfied with himself," he tells himself he should be kinder. Under pressure he acts foolishly, or with misplaced vehemence and tactless aggression. Though often too occupied with himself even to answer a friendly word from, *e.g.*, a server in a café, he is also very lonely. He has bad nerves, heart palpitations, head-aches, and will often flush with irrational guilt and self-condemnation. Worst of all he is intermittently "bitter and suspicious." He is neurotically quick to sense or imagine a threat, a slight, an insult, a look of blame and accusation, or a general hostility. He feels threatened, spied on, and is beset by endless misgivings and apprehensions. These feelings of course are concentrated during his relationship with Allbee who indeed does track him, spy on him, insult him, and invade his very being. But they are feelings he is habitually prone to.

His deeper fear comes from an uncertainty about

his position and stability in the cruel, indifferent chaos of the modern city. He puts it to himself this way: if his friends believe Allbee rather than him "then the turn he always feared had come and all good luck was cancelled and all favors melted away. . . . The currents had taken a new twist, and he was being hurried, hurried."[4] This sort of fear is endemic to life in the modern city. The securities of traditional status, identity, and position no longer obtain; all the old definitions are being washed away leaving only two categories— the successful, those who get away with it; and the failures, those who go under. At the outset Leventhal feels "I was lucky, I got away with it": but once in his life he too had drifted and come perilously close to that part of humanity "that did not get away with it—the lost, the outcast, the overcome, the effaced, the ruined."[5] Life in the modern city is like the three-legged race he once watched—an ungainly struggle to win at all costs. The struggle to win is ugly and undignified; but to lose, to fall, to be unlucky is terrible, and the threat of it is a constant source of nightmare and paranoia. Suspicion is bred by what Durkheim called the "anomie" of modern urban life;[6] the condition in which a man no longer feels maintained and identified by an established and enduring hierarchy, but set loose to fight and flounder in a turbulent sea of contesting greeds and fears. If a man is not sure who he is, nor who are his friends, then neither does he know his enemies: instead of living among neighbours, urban man has to struggle among crowds.

To drive home this basic atmosphere of alienation, insecurity, and the desperate, graceless motion and collision of this competitive, anomic age, Bellow power- fully evokes the crowded unrelated density of New York. At the start we see Leventhal squeezing through the shutting door of a bus, and he is forever knocking into things, banging himself against a packed and hampering environment. Even his clothes "bound and chafed him." Just to visit his sister-in-law he has to make an almost Dantesque ferry crossing: "The ferry crawled in the heat and blackness of the harbor. The mass of passengers on the open deck was still, like a crowd of souls, each concentrating on its destination."[7] The oppressive heat and noise of the city are recurringly brought home to us, as are its sudden savageries, its terrible loneliness. Bellow's Dreiseresque ability to pour the city on to his pages is used throughout with great effect: apartments, cafés, streets, cinemas, the changing lights of the city at night, glimpses through windows, the taste of an orange drink on a hot day, the soft noise of a waiter with saw-dust on his soles, the vast exotic unreality, and the miserable litter which intermix along with the "overwhelming human closeness and thickness," all this and more is made urgent and close for us so that at the end when Leventhal feels "that there was not a single part of him on which the whole world did not press with full weight" we are aware that it is the whole city life as well as the crushing presence of Allbee which he feels.

Now this atmosphere is crucial, not incidental, to the novel. For in this atmosphere of plenitude without meaning and crowdedness without coherence, the sense of human relationships is utterly uncertain and tenuous, while suspicions thrive on incomprehension and a lurking fear of vague powers which can destroy the individual in a moment. Allbee's anti-Semitism, his conviction that a conspiracy of Jews runs things, is only a more exaggerated paranoid vision of reality than Leventhal's conviction that there was a "black-list" which operated against him while he was unemployed. Likewise his father was convinced that enough money would free him from the power of the enemies. "And who were the

enemies? The world, everyone. They were imaginary."9
Leventhal's Jewish friends accuse him of "ghetto
psychology," and part of his sick bewilderment comes
from his inner struggle to find the right vision of reality
to accept. Most of the "versions of reality" in this book
stem from the fear and suspicion, the insecurity and sense
of threat, the mistrust of friends and intimations of
personal helplessness which modern urban life promotes.
This is the point behind the final Kafkaesque question
which is left hanging in the air at the end of the book:
"What's your idea of who runs things?" In the modern
world we are never quite sure, and our ignorance breeds
fear, and our fear engenders warped imaginings which
sever us from our fellow-men. It is in this atmosphere
that Leventhal comes to a "kind of recognition'" of
man's responsibilities, his relationship with other men.
The most important thing that happens to Leventhal
is that he is stirred out of his "indifference" and "recalcitrance" into a sense of general injustice and suffering, and thence to an awareness and confession of specific
blame and responsibility. Instead of timidly wrapping
himself up in his too-simple concept of "good luck"
he must emerge and be exposed to the problems of
environmental pressure, cruel chance, mixed deservings;
he must move beyond his paranoid sense of himself as
simple victim and realise that there are more complex
and subtler forms of "victimisation."

At first he tries to maintain that Allbee is responsible
for his own misfortune to make it bearable; but Allbee
knows that truth is harder than that.

But I'll tell you something. We do get it in the neck
for nothing, and there's no denying that evil is as
real as sunshine. Take it from me, I know what I'm
talking about. To you the whole thing is that I must
deserve what I get. That leaves your hands clean and
it's unnecessary for you to bother yourself.11

Gradually, as he digs down into his own mixed motives and looks over the past; as he hears the comments of other friends, and feels the force of Allbee's contentions, he realises: "He had contributed to it, though he had yet to decide to what extent he was to blame."[12] He never formulates the exact extent of his blame, but his confession of it is spelled out in his increasing weakness in the face of Allbee's intrusion into his life. Not that Allbee is entirely right: but he is not entirely wrong. And with that concession, no matter how tacitly made, Leventhal's safe and cautious life ("nothing dangerous and nothing glorious" as Allbee says) is rendered vulnerable to the onset of new and disturbing notions, some of them far-reaching and unanswerable. Problems which lead him to attempt to define what exactly it means to be "human."

The steps by which the unwelcome yet increasingly unresisted intimacy with Allbee is slowly forced on Leventhal are traced with subtle irresistability. Allbee persists in his visits, even to the point of moving in. And the feeling of closeness grows: "he had a strange, close consciousness of Allbee. . . a feeling of intimate nearness . . . the look of recognition Allbee bent on him duplicated the look in his own."[13] He lets him stay. He even helps him to bed when he is drunk. Revulsion for Allbee now alternates with something akin to real affection. At the same time Allbee is bringing chaos and mess into Leventhal's world. The flat gets increasingly dirty and disorderly. Allbee is somehow soiling the very centre of Leventhal's stable life. Yet Leventhal is unwilling and unable to deal with Allbee. It is possible, underneath all his weariness and helplessness, to see him permitting if not actually soliciting this unwanted disruption of his way of life. He even makes a tentative effort to help Allbee in a way which is tantamount to admitting that Allbee was correct in his version of Leventhal's guilt and debt. The showdown comes when he finds Allbee in his apartment making love to a strange woman. He throws them out in a spasm of violence and disgust. Indeed so harsh is he that he later feels remorse. But one feeling grows on him: "he felt simply that this disorder and upheaval was part of the price he was obliged to pay for his release."[14] The final stage of the dangerous involvement is reached when Allbee attempts suicide in such a way as to endanger Leventhal's life as well. Just in time Leventhal turns off the gas and ejects Allbee—this time for good. It would perhaps be too much to call this a symbolic death of the old self, but afterwards Leventhal certainly feels a different, healthier, calmer man. Born again, into a truer vision of reality. Allbee had said that a man could repent and utterly change his way of life: "You see, you have to get yourself so that you can't stand to keep on in the old way. . . . It takes a long time before you're ready to quit dodging. Meanwhile, the pain is horrible."[15] From one point of view the book follows Leventhal's dodging, his pain, and his change. This change hinges on a more profound realisation of the limits of the self and one's obligations to the rest of the world. And it should be stressed that Leventhal's growing insight into these problems is provoked mainly by the burdens imposed on him by his brother's family and Allbee, though it is perhaps accelerated and clarified by the remarks of the recurring domestic metaphysicians who inhabit Bellow's novels—marvellous talkers, all of them.

What, then has Leventhal learned? What new vision of man's involvement and complicity does he achieve? One extreme point of view is suggested by the old man in the cinema toilet who admires Boris Karloff because "he really understands what a mastermind is, a Law unto himself." But Karloff usually plays the part of an inhuman monster, and we may make the inference

that it is monstrous to try and be a law unto oneself.
The book had opened with Leventhal answering, if
grudgingly, a summons for aid from his sister-in-law,
and he instinctively deplores what he considers to be his
brother's neglect of his familial duty. Moreover, sheer
neutrality towards other people is shown up as abhorrent
by Allbee. He tells the story of the crowd on the subway
who saw a man injured by a train and did nothing to
help him because the policeman said they had to wait
for the ambulance. The man bled to death. Man can
be "penetrated by sympathy" as Leventhal is for his
nephew Philip, and even for Allbee; yet there is a strong
countering instinct to watch out only for the self and
disregard the claims of others. The human contains the
inhuman. As Leventhal realises when he compares the
glaring light of the city to "the yellow revealed in the
slit of the eye of a wild animal, say a lion, something
inhuman that didn't care about anything human
and yet was implanted in every human being too,
one speck of it. . . ."[16] It all comes back to the basic
question of man's need *for* and straining *against* limits.
Leventhal thinks at one point; "The peculiar thing
struck him that everything in nature was bounded;
trees, dogs, and ants didn't grow beyond a certain size.
'But we,' he thought, 'we go in all directions without
any limit'."[17] Yet another character says "men need a
harness" and the wise Schlossberg points out the
futility involved in a vague greed for limitless life by
underlining man's mortality. Man's aspiration is limitless, man is not:

There's a limit to me. But I have to be myself in
full. Which is somebody who dies, isn't it? That's
what I was from the beginning. I'm not three people,
four people. I was born once and I will die once.
You want to be two people? More than human?
Maybe it's because you don't know how to be one.[18]

Schlossberg is the man who voices the claims of a solving equilibrium: "It's bad to be less than human and it's bad to be more than human." And what is exactly human? He answers in terms which suggest that it depends on the value we attach to life:

> I am as sure about greatness and beauty as you are about black and white. If a human life is a great thing to me, it *is* a great thing. Do you know better? I'm entitled as much as you. And why be measly? Do you have to be? Is somebody holding you by the neck? Have dignity, you understand me? Choose dignity. Nobody knows enough to turn it down.[19]

The core of the problem is the self and its relation to the surrounding world. Should it seek for indefinite expansion, regarding the rest of the world as a tissue of chance, accident, and random unpredictability which has to be surmounted; should it conserve itself in caution and timidity? Be a spendthrift or a miser of the self? Here is a crucial meditation by Leventhal:

> Everybody wanted to be what he was to the limit. . . . There was something in people against sleep and dullness, together with the caution that led to sleep and dullness. Both were there, Leventhal thought. We were all the time taking care of ourselves, laying up, storing up, watching out on this side and on that side, and at the same time running, running desperately, running as if in an egg race with the egg in a spoon.[20]

Yet even this leaves something out. It leaves out that which drives Leventhal across on the ferry to do his brother's duty, it leaves out whatever it is that prompts him to lift the unwelcome and drunken Allbee to the comfort of a bed. It omits all that in a man which, no matter how reluctantly, comes to realise that all

men are somehow inter-related and therefore in some
way inter-responsible, sharing guilt and obligations in
ways too subtle for legislation. But sharing them,
nonetheless—as Leventhal's whole relationship with
Allbee demonstrates. Many men just want to be left
alone, too fearful to take on burdens, as Leventhal
realises; but he comes to a deeper wisdom: "he liked
to think 'human' meant accountable in spite of many
weaknesses—at the last moment, tough enough to
hold."[21] Man is born to flash, be himself to the limit,
but—"shoulders are from God and burdens too." On
one level the book is about the deeply ambiguous
relationship between Jew and non-Jew in modern
society. As Leslie Fiedler wrote: "At the moment when
the Jew in general, when the author himself as well as
his protagonist, have moved into situations of security,
however tenuous, inflicting injury in their scramble to
win that security, Bellow alone among our novelists
has had the imagination and the sheer nerve to portray
the Jew, the Little Jew, as victimizer as well as victim."[22]
But that "unforeseen partnership" (in Conrad's terms)
is paradigmatic of the relationship between man and
man—separated by strange fears and fierce competition,
yet locked together by a stranger love and sense of
obligation.

At the end of the book, Leventhal is portrayed as a
stronger, more relaxed, open figure; his obstinacy
mitigated, his recalcitrance softened. A man gains such
a strength after his way of life has been exposed to an
anarchic threat and has survived, enhanced by a deeper
wisdom. Yet there is something muffled and disappointing as well. Leventhal still embraces a view
of the world as pure chance: "It was a shuffle, all, all
accidental and haphazard,"[23] and Bellow does not
really show us a changed and wiser man, so much as
merely a more confident, less neurotic man. Has the

profound experience with Allbee simply been forgotten rather than absorbed? Their chance re-meeting in a theatre does little to clarify this point. There is, however, a hint as to where Bellow's subsequent interests might take him after the slightly exhausted, low-keyed ending of this powerful book. Leventhal meditates on the prevailing illusion that "at the start of life . . . a promise had been made." He likens this promise to a theatre ticket—everybody being predetermined to a certain place in the theatre of life. Then he rejects that comparison.

> There were more important things to be promised. Possibly there was a promise, since so many felt it. He himself was almost ready to affirm that there was. But it was misunderstood.[24]

An attempt to understand and follow out that implicit promise of life, sensed though unproven, was to follow.

REFERENCES

1. *T.V.*, p. 26.
2. *T.V.*, p. 29.
3. *T.V.*, p. 16.
4. *T.V.*, p. 83.
5. *T.V.*, p. 22.
6. See Emile Durkheim, *Suicide*, trans. J. Spaulding and G. Simpson, 1952.
7. *T.V.*, p. 59.
8. *T.V.*, p. 225.
9. *T.V.*, p. 100.
10. *T.V.*, p. 256.
11. *T.V.*, p. 130.
12. *T.V.*, p. 107.
13. *T.V.*, pp. 141-2.
14. *T.V.*, p. 238.
15. *T.V.*, p. 198.
16. *T.V.*, p. 48.
17. *T.V.*, p. 74.
18. *T.V.*, p. 223.
19. *T.V.*, p. 120.
20. *T.V.*, pp. 89-90.
21. *T.V.*, p. 137
22. Leslie Fiedler," Saul Bellow," 1957.
23. *T.V.*, p. 248.
24. *T.V.*, p. 249.

CHAPTER IV

IN AND OUT OF THE GAME

I touched all sides, and nobody knew where I belonged. I had no good idea of that myself.[1]

I didn't want to be what they made of me but wanted to please them. Kindly explain! An independent fate, and love too—what confusion![2]

You must take your chance on what you are. And you can't sit still. I know this double poser, that if you make a move you may lose but if you sit still you will decay.[3]

Before his next novel Bellow published three important short stories which in effect were monologues. They are written with a soaring highly-coloured vigour and a gay ferocity of speculation. In them it is possible to detect not only some key preoccupations and lines of inquiry but also Bellow's increasing preference for the narrative voice—musing, asking, recalling, asserting— over objective narration. In the first, "A Sermon by Doctor Pep,"[4] we are in the presence of a one-legged speaker in Bughouse Square, Chicago. His contention is: "Is there any real love short of eating?" And the burden of his sermon is a defence of the healthy, innocent appetite.

. . . the real and free presence of life is in the necessitous drink and the hungry bite of the man and woman who know how food is supplied and have met the debt of labor and acknowledgment. . . .

We can keep death too near us by secret care. It inhibits the bite, it poisons the mouthful, closes the indigestion and sends us to an early grave.

The healthy bite, the innocent predatory appetite, these are important notions for Bellow, reflected among other ways, in the significance he attaches to teeth in his novels. Both Augie and Henderson lose teeth as they bite at life in their hunger and longing. Somewhat atavistic, he suggests that civilisation with its stress on gentleness, restraint, order, and the disguise of appetite, actually devours itself at the same time as it may be moving towards something far more monstrous than honest hunting and devouring. Doctor Pep mentions Auschwitz.

A related point is made by Weyl in his talk to Scampi on a hospital balcony in "The Trip to Galena."[5] He is, like Augie March, surrounded by people who want to plan his life for him. He stays unattached. His story is about a visit to his sister's fiancé's dull, respectable household. He rebels against their suffocating stress on manners and politeness:

Nobody takes that seriously any more, the dance of conduct. There're other steps that have been crowding our legs. We're more and more in the open of our natures, nearer and nearer to the original personal quality in people. . . . the next conduct will have to come from the heart, from attachment to life despite the worst it has shown us, and it has shown us just about everything.

The important idea is the need to get back and down to the original quality of people, of life; to rediscover its innate nobility and promise.

In the "Address by Gooley MacDowell to the Hasbeens Club of Chicago"[6] Bellow offers a third attack

on the excesses of civilisation—this time on the over-
developed consciousness of self induced by too much
stress on ideas and the abnormally developed intelligence
"Because this kind of consciousness can be like sharing
a bed with a pal who is running a high fever, and at
last you would rather shake down on the hard floor
of fact, where no humanity is, in the fair cool space of
vectors and the topless tent of laws, open to the universe.
That's for removal from the burning *me*." He ponders
why this should be, dwelling on the barrenness of much
thought.

> But a person can no longer keep up; and plenty are
> dying of good ideas. . . . Look at us, deafened, hamper-
> ed, obstructed, impeded, impaired and bowel-gutted
> with wise counsel and good precept, and the more
> plentiful our ideas the worse out headaches. So we ask,
> will some good creature pull out the plug and ease our
> disgusted hearts a little? We are not free to use it,
> that is why advice is a loaded burden.

Like many other Bellow characters, it is the sense of
curtailment and restriction which prompts MacDowell
to his diagnosis:

> Intelligent? What for, you subject-man and personal
> ant, when you're so much at the mercy and soldered
> up inside determinations.

He too believes in "feelings of being that go beyond and
beyond all I ever knew or thought, and a massiver
existence of man" but he cannot see that the sterile
proliferation of impotent ideas by the cramped, self-
correcting, self-mutilating mind is the way to arrive at
them. But ideas broached in a sermon, an address, a
hospital-balcony reminiscence are one thing, and the
discovery and validation of them through frictional
contact with the world is another. Clearly Bellow needed
a character who, like Dr Pep, had "hopes of brilliancy"

and a true innocence of appetite; who, like Weyl, would not allow others to plan his life for him and repudiated sadness and despair in the belief that life has a "nobility" if we can learn to approach the "original personal quality in people"; and who, like Gooley MacDowell, wanted to find out what his real nature was, not through intellectual self-preoccupation, but by the following out of inclination, the refusal of arrest and privation, and the insistence that truly valuable knowledge must bestow happiness and be an aid rather than a burden to the self. And this character would have to explore the promise of life by a genuine exposure to it, an uncompromising immersion in it. Thus Augie March seems the logical outcome of a distinctive trend—the necessary tester of a series of deepening convictions.

When *The Adventures of Augie March* came out in 1953, Robert Penn Warren made an interesting point in his review. Saying that Bellow's first novels were written in "the Flaubert-James" tradition, muted, tightly organised within a rigid form, he went on: "It would be interesting to know what led Saul Bellow to turn suddenly from a method in which he was expert and in which, certainly, he would have scored triumphs."[7] Now we might answer with Ihab Hassan that in portraying a victim who is ruled by necessity a writer will be led to a closed form, while in following up a rebel, who gives the illusion of escaping from necessity, he will be drawn to an open form.[8] But this is not the whole of it. In an interview of the same year Bellow talked about the writing of the book. "The great pleasure of the book was that it came easily. All I had to do was be there with buckets to catch it. That's why the form is loose." And he goes on to complain that the novel has been imitating poetry far too much. How? "In its severity and style and devotion to exact form. In the great period of the novel, the novelist didn't care—there was a great mass of sand

B—D

and gravel: there was diversity of scene, a large number of characters." Concern with form, he implies, involves a neglect of contemporary reality. So—"I kicked over the traces, wrote catch-as-catch can, picaresque. I took my chance."[9] A later article made the point more uncompromisingly. "I think the novelists who take the bitterest view of our modern conditions make the most of the art of the novel." Then he quotes Flaubert who said "I abhor ordinary existence. . . . I am turning towards a kind of aesthetic mysticism," and adds, "the majority of modern novelists have followed the standard of Flaubert, the aesthetic standard." "Disappointment with its human material is built into the contemporary novel. It is assumed that society cannot give the novelist suitable themes and characters. Therefore the important humanity of the novel must be the writer's own. His force, his virtuosity, his powers of poetry, his reading of fate are at the center of the book.[10] Clearly Bellow wanted to counter-act this "aesthetic standard" with its implicitly negative attitude to life. Of course, there is much that is abhorrent in modern life. But we must beware a complacent despair. "The enormous increases in population seem to have dwarfed the individual. So have modern physics and astronomy. But we may be somewhere between a false greatness and a false insignificance. At least we can stop misrepresenting ourselves to ourselves and realize that the only thing we can be in this world is human. We are temporarily miracle-sodden and feeling faint."[11] What Bellow so often insists is that the artist's imagination need not be swamped by modern life, nor need it turn away from it. There is always the chance of a new containing order and a love that can span and support.

Many events fall upon us, assail us with claims on our time and our judgment; waves of disintegrative details wash over us and threaten to wear away all sense of order and proportion. The novelist begins at a great depth of distraction and difficulty. . . . A novelist begins with disorder and disharmony, and he goes toward order by an unknown process of the imagination. . . . No one knows what the power of the imagination comes from or how much distraction it can cope with. We are told it has reached its limit. The distraction is supposed to be too broad for love and too deep for beauty and too agonizing for order.[12]

He admits that sometimes one feels that all the distractions of modern life seem like an attempt to obliterate the individual being, and that sometimes in the streets one gets the impression that "the energies of the population have been withdrawn to mass activity, industry, and money": but then he asks "Can the intellectual asthetic, moral genius of the human race have come to a stop? That's impossible." He then goes on to point out that "impotence has received more attention from modern writers than any other subject." By "impotence" he also means "the loss or defect of the sympathetic power, the failure of feeling," and he cites among others Oblomov, Moreau, Captain Ahab, Clym Yeobright, the narrators of James's "Beast in the Jungle" and Dostoevsky's *Notes from Underground*, and Leopold Bloom. "They all tell the same story. The dread is great, the soul is small; man might be godlike but he is wretched; the heart should be open but it is sealed by fear."[13] Bellow is intent on resisting the low view of contemporary man for many reasons, but for one especially. He refuses to accept the validity and finality of the "agreed picture," in this case "the agreed picture" that "we are a mass civilization, doomed to be shallow and centerless."

Why were we born? What are we doing here? Where

are we going? In its eternal naïveté the imagination keeps coming back to these things. It does this when we have an agreed picture and when we haven't. For it isn't an agreed picture that makes man interesting to himself. It isn't history and it isn't culture: the interest is intrinsic.[14]

Agreed pictures, or what he elsewhere calls "systems"[15] tend to make us "resist new forms of reality." So the novelist must get beyond systems and agreed pictures and "find enduring intuitions of what things are real and what things are important. His business is with these enduring intuitions which have the power to recognise occasions of suffering or occasions of happiness, in spite of all distortion and blearing."[16] More important, when all the readings of the modern age are belittling and condemnatory, the novel must continue to care, to believe, to "manifest love." "We are called upon to preserve our humanity in circumstances of rapid change and movement. I do not see what else we can do than refuse to be condemned with a time or a place. We are not born to be condemned but to live."[17]

These foregathered statements by Bellow should help us to understand the shape, movement, and temper of Augie March's book. When the book appeared, in 1953, it was greeted very enthusiastically (it received the National Book Award), and critics inevitably commented on its picaresque nature, approving its euphoric variety. And variety is indeed offered us with upwards of eighty characters passing before us, each with his or her distinctive, if momentary, vividness. Incidents and episodes are too numerous to summarise, moving from pre-war Chicago, through Mexico, on to the War and finishing in post-war Europe. And Augie himself looks very like a picaresque hero, to such an extent that Leslie Fiedler saw him as a unique combination of the picaresque *schlimazl* and Huck Finn. Yet there is an important difference to be noted. The traditional picaresque hero is himself, fully formed, from the outset; his adventures multiply incidents without issuing in wisdom. But Augie is in fact trying to discover what he himself is, in the deepest sense. The structure of the book, therefore, despite its air of improvisation, its tone of strolling, arbitrary recall, is directed and controlled by deeper concerns. Incidents which seem random, grabbed at for their own sake, reveal a retrospective relevance as certain themes and lines of inquiry emerge. The adventures turn out to have contained a quest.

"I have always tried to become what I am," says Augie: of course this involves a risk—"what if what I am by nature isn't good enough?"—but "You must take your chance on what you are. . . . It is better to die what you are than to live a stranger forever."[18] What is the true self; how navigate it through life? These two questions are responsible for the dimension of the book which transcends the traditionally "picaresque." Augie's quest for true identity and a proper fate is rendered peculiarly difficult by the nature of the world he is born into and has to move through. *Life Among the Machiavellians* the book was to be called, and that last key word appears at the start and near the end of the novel. Grandma Lausch, the first person who tries to shape Augie's life for him (and incidentally one of the most impressive portraits in the book) is described as "one of those Machiavellis of small street and neighbourhood that my young years were full of."[19] And at the end, after Augie has barely escaped from the lunatic Basteshaw who has plans to change the whole human race, he comments: "To tell the truth, I'm good and tired of all these big personalities, destiny moulders, and heavy-water brains, Machiavellis and wizard evildoers, big-wheels and imposers-upon, absolutists."[20] There are different types and modes of manipulation at work in the world of the book: instruction (Grandma Lausch), advice (Einhorn), adoption (Mrs Renling), familial coercion (Simon), seduction (Thea), and violence (Basteshaw); power and influence may be exercised for different motives and the manipulators may vary enormously in human quality. But such is the world of the book; the individual self continually enticed or threatened, pushed or drawn by other people's versions of what life is for and how it should be led.

At the crudest level people can be divided according to "whether they screwed or were screwed, whether they themselves did the manipulating or were roughly handled, tugged, and bobbled by their fates."[21] It is a world of materialists, pushing, bullying, and exploiting for the sake of more money. Not to make material progress is to be a fool. Simon's brother follows this ethic to its logical conclusion and he starkly reveals how it brutalises a man and devalues his life. But beyond material exploitation there are innumerable other forms of imposition. At a higher level there are the word-mongers, the people who try to impose a theory, a version, a system of life on Augie. He feels that "of all the impositions this was the worst imposition. Not just to be as they make you but to feel as they dictate."[22] Particularly if the feeling is pessimistic, or the theory a low one. Of course Augie often learns from "those persons who persistently arise before me with life counsels and illumination"; and one of the exciting aspects of the book is the dance of ideas it sets in motion and the kaleidoscope of theories it reveals. Nevertheless, although Bellow is clearly using some of these speakers to display and explore some of his own ideas, by the end of the book Augie says with some weariness "Why did I always have to fall among theoreticians!";[23] and at one stage of his adventures he says with some resignation "After much making with sense, it's senselessness you submit to."[24] In this world of exploiters and theoreticians Augie's principal ambition is to resist total manipulation: "My pride has always been hurt by not being able to give an account of myself and always being manipulated. Reality comes from giving an account of yourself."[25] That is to say he does not want to be merely a determined creature, passive to all manner of coercive pressure; rather, he wants to be necessary. He wants to resist what one character calls "*moha* . . . meaning opposition of the finite. It is the Bronx cheer of the conditioning forces. Love is the only answer to *moha*, being infinite."[26] The conditioning forces are extensive and powerful in the world of the book just as the conditioning people are thick around Augie. And in such a world, dense, impinging and constricting, it is a difficult task to sing the "song of myself." Augie's book records his attempts to sing that song, and the difficulties attendant on that ambition.

For all the bravado and independence of his tone, Augie in fact is a very passive character, amenable to suggestions and offers, pliant, with apparently little momentum of his own. He seldom initiates any course of action, seldom makes a positive, forward-moving, creative decision or choice. For his employment he is totally reliant on the offers and ideas of other people. Simon gets him a job selling papers and later takes him into his coal yard, Einhorn gets him a job with a luxury dog service, Padilla teaches him to steal books, Ruber offers him the paint-selling job, Thea takes him to Mexico, Mimi pushes him into the W.P.A., Mintouchian gets him his dubious post-war business job in Europe. And so on. Since he cannot find anything to warrant "singleness of purpose," he remains "diffuse." Thea, a sharp critic, tells him he simply plays everyone's game, endlessly adjusting in order to be obliging, but with

no real staying power. "You get tired easily." People
are "adoptive" towards him, they try to fit him into their
schemes, as Stella points out: so, much of Augie's
evasion, his endless opting-out and moving-on, can be
seen as a strenuous effort to avoid being defined by
external pressure. But this passivity is very extreme.
When Frazer offers him a strange job, involved with
Trotsky, he prays God to "keep me from being sucked
into another of those great currents where I can't be
myself."[27] This suggests a docility to suggestion and a
plasticity to the shufflings and dealings of chance which
sometimes makes one wonder whether Augie has the
strength to find and be himself. True, he resists final
commitment and refuses ultimate assent to any of the
proferred involvements or imposed situations, and this
very energy of evasion is a positive gesture on behalf of
the elusive, wary, ever-mobile self—avoiding fixity,
arrest, and rigidity, refusing to jell in any of the debased
moulds of the age, asserting fluid unattachment as a
virtue, and retaining disponibility at all costs. When the
game is such a basically corrupt game—as it is in Augie's
world—then every entry into it must be followed by some
effort of self-extraction. Hence the recurring rhythm of
the book: a drifting into things finally stopped by a
sudden digging in of the heels or a sudden flight from
attachment; either way a repudiation of commitment.
And the end of the books seems less like a victory of love
over *moha* than a weary succumbing to the vortex of the
game. Apparently Augie can only define and maintain
himself through negative acts. It is worth recalling Peer
Gynt who exhibited a comparable self-preserving adapt-
ability, who never took the irrevocable step of a commitment which could not be reversed, and who finished up
a creature of many layers and no centre. Critics noticed
this aspect of Augie: Robert Penn Warren suggested
that the conception of the character might have been

"stronger if Augie had been given the capacity for deeper commitments for more joy and sorrow,"[28] and Leslie Fiedler, noting the un-Jewish nature of the book "in being concerned not with a man's rise but with his evasion of rising," pointed out that Augie's refusal of binding allegiances and denial of base values is made in the interests of "only a limitless disponibility guarded like a treasure."[29] Augie touches all sides and never finds out where he belongs, for in this book there is a good deal of touching but very little proper holding, and while people are in constant collision they almost never establish relationships. And in this atomistic hugger-mugger Augie never really finds anything to warrant a positive commitment. So Augie "circles" since he cannot identify with the "directions" chosen by other people.

Circling is one better than dangling, but despite Augie's joy in free movement there is that in him which yearns to alight, to make the valid, significant, self-focussing act. But rather like the eagle he trains, when he does make his pounce he disappoints others because he is not total and violent enough. Which may testify to a superior humanity—for Augie will do things for love he will not do for ambition—and a way of out-witting *his* would-be trainers. But it also shows that he can find nothing worth alighting for. The eagle's refusal of a predatory role only seems like cowardice to people who live by rapine. Still it *is* disappointing not to see the eagle fulfilling himself with assurance and dedication. Thus Augie himself. Einhorn tells him "You've got *opposition* in you. You don't slide through everything. You just make it look so." And at the same time Augie discovers his "great desire to offer resistance and to say 'No'!". "No, I didn't want to be what he called determined. I never had accepted determination and wouldn't become what other people wanted to make of

me."[30] But his opposition usually takes the form of a
last moment refusal to be totally trained—just as the
eagle is domesticated but finally baulks at killing the
lizards.

He has one positive scheme—to set up a school of
his own so that he never has to "loan myself again to
any other guy's scheme."[31] But that comes to nothing
and at the end of the book Stella is "carrying" him.
He clings on to his freedom, refusing to become a type,
refusing to be recruited to other peoples' version of
"what's real," but for what? "If I didn't have money
or profession or duties, wasn't it so that I could be free,
and a sincere follower of love?"[32] But he isn't that and
he knows he isn't. He seems only capable of temporary
emotional attachments, brief momentary intensities.
As in much American fiction there is no deep sense of
continuity of feeling or duration of relationship. Augie
himself realises "I couldn't be hurt enough by the fate
of other people."[33] His interest is really in his independent
fate, with a paradoxical yearning to find a true and
committing love—a common paradox in American
literature. His difficulty is in finding a focus. "I longed
very much, but I didn't understand for what"[34] (like
Dreiser's Carrie). Clem Tambow calls him an angel but,
accurately, tells him he is not "concrete" enough. His
aspirations are too general. Clem's diagnosis is central.
"What I guess about you is that you have a nobility syndrome. You can't adjust to the reality situation."[35]
Augie agrees: he will not accept a disappointed view of
life, he refuses to "offer to die." Opposition. But is it
enough to help him navigate his life? All too often Augie
fails to get beyond the state he himself describes: "All was
vague on my side and yet it was also very stubborn."[36]
Yet something can be affirmed by what William James
called "the self-governing resistance of the ego to the
world," and in the course of Augie's various moves

towards experience and moves away from regimentation and commitment, a wisdom and a sense of positive values does emerge.

Bellow, like Padilla, is fascinated by "the little individual who tries to have a charge counter to the central magnetic one and dance his own dance on the periphery,"[37] for such a person is insisting on his right to an individual destiny. That is why Augie is so consistently interested in the question of fate. The common view is that in the modern world people are like particles —"they may have functions but certainly lack fates." But Augie is stubborn, if vague: "Nevertheless I stand by my idea of a fate. For which a function is a substitution of a deeper despair."[38] Augie leaves situation after situation because it does not offer a good enough fate. But what is a man's fate, and how does he find it? Augie starts the book by quoting Heraclitus: "a man's character is his fate," and he ends it by simply inverting the idea: "it is obvious that this fate, or what he settled for, is also his character. And since I have never had any place of rest, it should follow that I have trouble being still, and furthermore my hope is based upon getting to be still so that the axial lines can be found."[39] Augie has not found that stillness by the end and the axial lines are more talked about than discovered. But the need for a fate, as opposed to a function, has been pressed home very powerfully. What is uncertain is the relation between the individual and the larger laws of life. Augie is quite firm: "I want to obey those laws. . . . I'm not trying to get out from under. I never did try."[40] It is hard to see which laws he is transcending and which he capitulates to. In one passage Augie tries to clarify these problems and paradoxes—paradoxes suggested by the comparison between his brother who is a dynamic man of force and decision, and who yet seems increasingly conditioned and enslaved, and Augie who is given to passivity and indolence and yet retains at least a measure of detachment from the determining forces of the world.

> I have a feeling about the axial lines of life, with respect to which you must be straight or else your existence is merely clownery, hiding tragedy. I must have had a feeling since I was a kid about these axial lines which made me want to have my existence on them, and so I have said "no" like a stubborn fellow to all my persuaders, just on the obstinacy of my memory of those lines, never entirely clear. But lately I have felt those thrilling lines again. When striving stops, there they are as a gift.[41]

Augie's attempts to find a high and distinctive fate are hardly successful, and indeed at times he tires of the pilgrimage. But he has moved towards a form of reconciliation, not with society but with life itself. He can look back at his life as a series of errors, but he has gained the saint's intimation "that blessedness covers the whole Creation but covers it thicker in some places than in others." And he calls it *"amor fati . . .* or mysterious adoration of what occurs."[42]

One can bestow a value on life by adopting an attitude of positive and reverent acceptance towards it: Augie's main gesture of affirmation is his refusal to "live a disappointed life." Because the terrible fact is, as Augie knows, that life does "end with so many disappointments in the essential."[43] And his quest is to discover how most positively to cope with this fact. We are not, cannot be, living "at the dwarf end of all times," so there must still be occasions of redeeming greatness and nobility. Even though Augie starts surrounded by "deep city vexation" instead of the lucid air of ancient Greece, even though he starts his adult career in a poolroom, he still insists on inquiring "what can that lead to of the highest."[44] He insists on "this universal eligibility to be noble,"[45] and even though the human spirit has a more difficult task in this more crowded, more corrupt world, "there may gods turn up anywhere."[46] This is one reason why Augie so consistently compares his characters to figures from myth, history, and classical legend. Partly, perhaps, to suggest a humorous discrepancy, but more certainly to suggest that great men and significant events are not over for all time. Einhorn's adventures prompt Augie to think of "the old tale of Croesus," just as the old man himself is elevated to equality with Caesar, Machiavelli, and Ulysses. The moral is simply this: "we all catch up with legends, more or less."[47]

The nobility of life may not be immediately or easily demonstrable, but—the only hope is hope. At least, Augie never gets bored for long. Hence the ending of the book. Augie can scarcely be said to be leading a noble life or following a distinctive fate. Yet as he stands in the cold winter fields with the old French maid Jacqueline, whose dream is to visit Mexico, Augie can make a tentative and provisional gesture of affirmation. Surrounded as he is by evidence of the relentless, non-human destructiveness of nature, he nevertheless starts laughing. The *animal ridens* rises up.

What's so laughable, that a Jacqueline, for instance, as hard used as that by rough forces, will still refuse to lead a disappointed life? Or is the laugh at nature —including eternity—that it thinks it can win over us and the power of hope? Nah, nah! I think. It never will. But that probably is the joke, on one or the other, and laughing is an enigma that includes both.[48]

And Augie bows himself out as "a sort of Columbus of those near-at-hand," adding as a final parting ironic gesture: "I may well be a flop at this line of endeavour.

Columbus too thought he was a flop, probably, when they sent him back in chains. Which didn't prove there was no America."[49] Augie has not really found any new continents of life's possibilities—indeed we leave him in a very old one, tied to a corrupt business and a deceptive wife. His farewell is not a consummation, but a gesture—countenancing hope, refusing despair. Not dying amidst the deathly evidence.

For all this, the end of the book is unsatisfying in certain ways. Many critics felt this even while eulogising the book as a whole. Feidler said the book "does not know how to end; shriller and shriller, wilder and wilder, it finally whirls apart in a frenzy of fake euphoria and exclamatory prose."[50] Marcus Klein felt that the book "does not earn that leap into faith"[51] which is asserted in connexion with the discovery of the axial lines. Richard Chase felt that at the end of the book Augie is left wavering, no longer sure that varietism and freedom will lead him to "individual autonomy,"[52] and Robert Penn Warren asked "is his comic and heroic philosophy quite enough, even for Augie? Augie himself, I hazard, scarcely thinks so."[53] Certainly the affirmation is very vague and generalised. Augie has not really come to the point of any specific, concrete valid commitment or reconciliation: the book can never end as long as the oscillation between accommodation and alienation is uninterrupted, and the marriage with Stella is really only a cutting off—in no sense a consummation or resolution. Now of course, this is perfectly honest on the part of the author. What one does feel is that Augie's larky freedom, his lucky breaks, the extraordinary offers made to him, the chances for evasion and moving on that come to him—all these are somehow a bit contrived, a way of removing him to some degree from the relentless pressures of big-city determinism. His assertion that man is "only ostensibly born to remain in specified limits"[54] is a familiar idea in Bellow's work: but before any valuable allegiances can be established some sense of some limits must be learned. With only a sense of limitless possibilities there can be no stopping point—one will circle forever. And despite the entanglements we see Augie involved in, at the end of the book one does not feel that he has really come to firm grips with a concrete environment. His affirmations tend to skirt "the opposition of the finite" rather than meet it. Sometimes the wisdom seems to be superadded to the adventures rather than an outcome of them, for Augie seldom stays still long enough to learn the lessons of freedom and fate which he is aware of in outline. Something of the desolation and disappointment which underlie the affirmative ending stems from the pervading feeling that Augie has never totally faced up to things, never really seen any one issue through, and that even he is not quite sure what positive value there was in that disponibility he spent so long so jealously preserving. As Robert Penn Warren pointed out, "it is hard to give substance to a man who has no commitments,"[55] and by the end Augie has come to seem rather light, somewhat blurred and insubstantial, a diffuse presence rather than an individual person.

But he does have a voice, the voice which is the style of the book. And this voice, this style, does communicate the identity of Augie March. From the start we know that this is a Whitmanesque voice which has renounced all attempts at any cautious Flaubertian accuracy of description. "I am an American, Chicago born . . . and go at things as I have taught myself, free-style, and will make the record in my own way . . . . Everybody knows there is no fineness or accuracy of suppression; if you hold down one thing you hold down the adjoining."[56] Augie is out to suppress nothing, rather to

include everything, relevant and adjoining, that has
touched him. The style is hospitable, omnivorous,
assimilatory. And if there is sometimes something hectic
in the manic inclusiveness there is also clearly some
awe, some love in the almost desperate wideness of
embrace. Augie digresses and jumps, freely associates
and anticipates, amasses anecdote, character, event,
idea, conversation in a tumult of improvised semi-
poetry. Things and people are poured out rather than
narrated and one of the abiding impressions is of a vast
unrelated abundance—everything thrown together so
unpredictably or moving by so fast that there is no time
for precision and analysis; Augie can only sweep up
great handfuls in a tumult of words.

Sometimes, indeed, the lavishing of epithets is excessive—*e.g.*, Jacqueline's "freezing, wavering, mascara-
lined, goblin, earnest and disciplinarian, membranous,
and yet gorgeous face."[57] But the style as a whole is
very American in its preference for wonder, enumera-
tion, a welcoming inclusiveness, a generosity in the
face of plentitude, as opposed to those modes which
select, re-arrange, and analyse. And yet just as Augie
touches things and people on all sides without any real
deep allegiance, so his voice, his words touch everything,
pick everything up, without seeming to take their full
weight and pressure. The world of the book is teeming
yet oddly impermanent, incomparably vivid and
physical yet, after the tremendous opening chapters,
touched by insubstantiality. Augie's voice, with its
wide-ranging delight and wondering openness to experience, does justify the move towards wisdom and affirmation; yet it also reveals what his fate reveals, namely
that he has not yet learned a way of significantly and
confidently relating to any one aspect of the world.
The style like the man, is a circling one. Fascinated
by life's possibilities they both yet fail of true attachment.

REFERENCES

1. *A.M.*, p. 113.
2. *A.M.*, p. 401.
3. *A.M.*, p. 485.
4. "A sermon by Doctor Pep," May 1949.
5. "The Trip to Galena," 1950.
6. "Address by Gooley Mac-Dowell to the Hasbeens Club of Chicago," 1951.
7. *New Republic*, 2 Nov. 1953.
8. Ihab Hassan, *Radical Innocence*, 1961, p. 123.
9. Harvey Breit, "Talk with Saul Bellow," *New York Times Book Review*, 20 Sep. 1953.
10. "The Sealed Treasure," 1960.
11. *Op. cit.*
12. "Distractions of a Fiction Writer," 1957.
13. *Op. cit.*
14. *Op. cit.*
15. "The Writer and the Audience," in *Perspectives*, 9, Autumn 1954.
16. *Op. cit.*
17. "How I wrote Augie March's Story," in *New York Times Book Review*, 31 Jan. 1954.
18. *A.M.*, p. 485.
19. *A.M.*, p. 4.
20. *A.M.*, p. 524.
21. *A.M.*, p. 73.
22. *A.M.*, p. 417.
23. *A.M.*, p. 503.
24. *A.M.*, p. 390.
25. *A.M.*, p. 450.
26. *A.M.*, p. 450.
27. *A.M.*, p. 416.
28. "The Man with no Commitments," in *New Republic*, 2 Nov, 1953.
29. "Saul Bellow," 1957.
30. *A.M.*, p. 117.
31. *A.M.*, p. 456.
32. *A.M.*, p. 401.
33. *A.M.*, p. 453.
34. *A.M.*, p. 84.
35. *A.M.*, p. 434.
36. *A.M.*, p. 252.
37. *A.M.*, p. 191.
38. *A.M.*, p. 516.
39. *A.M.*, p. 316.
40. *A.M.*, p. 483.
41. *A.M.*, pp. 454-5.
42. *A.M.*, p. 527.
43. *A.M.*, p. 412.
44. *A.M.*, p. 84.
45. *A.M.*, p. 29.
46. *A.M.*, p. 260.
47. *A.M.*, p. 333.
48. *A.M.*, p. 536.
49. *Ibid.*
50. "Saul Bellow," 1957.
51. "A Discipline of Nobility," in *Kenyon Review*, Spring 1962.
52. "The Adventures of Saul Bellow," 1959.
53. "The Man with no Commitments," 1953.
54. *A.M.*, p. 240.
55. "The Man with no Commitments," 1953.
56. *A.M.*, p. 3.
57. *A.M.*, p. 535.

CHAPTER V

THE WORLD'S BUSINESS

Uch! How they love money, thought Wilhelm. They adore money! Holy money! Beautiful money! It was getting so that people were feeble-minded about everything except money. While if you didn't have it you were a dummy, a dummy! You had to excuse yourself from the face of the earth. Chicken! That's what it was. The world's business. If only he could find a way out of it.[1]

Augie was never really trapped. He met obstacles and got entangled with encumbrances, but so many freakish opportunities for evasion presented themselves that he never really got locked fast in the world's embrace. He is perhaps a little *too* larky and boisterous—as though he had never really met with those remorseless factors in a man's life which can bruise, cripple, and arrest. If his affirmation sounds a little unearned, it is because he does not give the impression of having encountered the sort of opposition which makes such affirmation difficult. The world is not heavy on him, and in consequence he sometimes seems a rather light-weight figure. In his next important work, the *novella Seize the Day*, Bellow portrayed a character on whom the world's weight is heavy indeed; a man "stripped and kicked out," spurned by his father, persecuted by his wife, and victimised by a confidence trickster. Tommy Wilhelm also lives in a world of Machiavellians but this time they exert a real and sinister power and by the end of the book he is genuinely exhausted, bowed down, at the end of his tether. Augie saw his life as a series of mistakes but his mistakes did not catch up with him. Wilhelm's life is also a sequence of errors: but every one serves to limit his freedom, curtail his choices, corner him, and slow him down till we find him choking, constricted, and all but unable to move. Tommy Wilhelm meets the world's opposition full face.

When Bellow published *Seize the Day* in book form in 1956, he included with it three short stories which should be mentioned here as they not only show up some of the themes preoccupying Bellow at this time, but also touch, in different ways, on a major concern of *Seize the Day*—the terrible and ubiquitous power of money. "A Father-to-Be"[2] is an amusing and perceptive story about a young research chemist going to visit his fiancée who suddenly sees in the man sitting next to him on the subway a terrible premonition of what his own son might be like—dull, complacent, smug, *bourgeois*. He resents the idea that the life force uses people so indifferently, he dislikes the idea of being an instrument, his own unique value negated in the onward rush of mere preservation of the species. Like all Bellow protagonists he resists the feeling of being helplessly involved in determinism.

Resolved to assert his own right to exist he arrives at his fiancée's house in a mood of aggression, bent on holding out against the pressures pushing him from all sides. She, however, all tender and soft, persuades him to let her wash his hair and in the warm engulfing suds his resolution melts away and he accepts his role. Whether this is an ennervated capitulation or a courageous assumption of life's duties is not discussed: the comic insight into how easily we can be led to renounce our ambitions for individual density is the dominant note. But there is an important passage. The hero is meditating in a drug store, thinking over his many financial obligations:

Money surrounds you in life as the earth does in death.
Superimposition is the universal law. Who is free?
No one is free. Who has no burdens? Everyone is
under pressure. The very rocks, the waters of the
earth, beasts, men, children—everyone has some
weight to carry. . . . The notion that all were under
pressure and affliction, instead of saddening him,
had the opposite influence. It put him in a wonderful
mood. It was extraordinary how happy he became
and, in addition, clear-sighted.

Is man born to be free, or born to be burdened? If
burdened, how can he achieve a mode of acceptance
and affirmation which will raise him above a mere
pawn of necessity? Here is a central concern for Bellow.
The next story "Looking for Mr. Green"[3] dated
from 1951 and is a really suggestive parable of the
Depression period. A man who has to deliver relief
cheques in a Negro district finds it is oddly difficult to
locate a certain Mr Green. The whole evocation of
Chicago in its wintry desolation is very impressive;
and the search for Mr Green, the suspicious unhelpful-
ness of the other slum dwellers, very powerfully brings
home the feeling of how easily a man might simply
disappear, fading away out of his identity in obscure
anonymity until his name no longer corresponds to
any abiding reality. Finally, after an encounter with a
drunken naked Negress, he gives her the cheque to give
to Mr Green and consoles himself with the thought that
"after all he *could* be found" even though he has not
been able to establish his reality personally. Here the
problem turns on the misery and ugliness of the modern
world where, as an old Negro says, "the only thing is
money. That's the only sunbeams, money." Such a world
is trapped among appearances; there must be another
superior, enduring form of reality. But meanwhile people

are held down and things are held in place by need.
People have to "labor in the fallen world of appearances" where need and difficulties and miseries are
real enough to demand a maximum of attention. And
yet, they cannot be the only realities, even in the middle
of the Depression. Like other Bellow figures, Grebe
wants to affirm a deeper reality, without denying the
impinging weight of the world of appearances.

The third story, "The Gonzaga Manuscripts,"[4]
concerns another quest. Clarence Feiler searches for some
lost manuscripts of Gonzaga, a Spanish poet now dead,
whom he admires. He admires Gonzaga's work because
it expresses content with simply being a "creature,"
accepting the world without wishing to change it, or
berate it, without valuing his art above life itself.
He was "natural" and in the modern world it is very
hard to be natural. Feiler tries to conduct the search in
the spirit of Gonzaga, but in modern Spain no one is
interested in Gonzaga's work—it is all money. Even the
one sympathetic girl he meets is involved in getting
cheap pesetas on the black market. One old family
simply make jokes about the atomic bomb, and the
man most likely to be able to help Feiler thinks he is
"a financier" interested in his pitchblende mine.
"Pitchblende has uranium in it. Uranium is used in
atom bombs." No one can imagine he is genuinely
interested in Gonzaga's poetry. In this world the
dominant values are money values; the profit motive
is uppermost and money has become intimately involved
with man's most destructive instincts as represented by
the atomic bomb. Clarence flees, But in *Seize the Day*
there is no chance of flight for Tommy Wilhelm.

He is a complete victim of "the world's business" and
it has driven him to the wall. Money pervades the world
of the *novella*—"There's money everywhere"—it has
reached down into people's hearts until they are cynical,

and it has corroded human relations to the point where financial success and failure can determine the attitude a father takes to his son, a wife to a husband. When the book opens we see Tommy brought to the point where he has no more money and his "obligations" threaten to destroy him. He has learnt some of the harder facts about "freedom." "Don't talk to me about being free. A rich man may be free on an income of a million net. A poor man may be free because nobody cares what he does. But a fellow in my position has to sweat it out until he drops dead."[5] This is more in line with hard reality than Augie's euphoric hurdling. But although Tommy is helpless to remove himself from this money world where suspicion, cynicism, and exploitation dominate people, he is at least not at home in it, and he fears its adverse effects. "Too much of the world's business done. Too much falsity. He had various words to express the effect this had on him. Chicken! Unclean! Congestion! he exclaimed in his heart. Rat race! Phony! Murder! Play the game! Buggers!"[6] He feels congestion and pressure to a degree which Augie never does, and indeed the movement of the book—which covers only one day— is from a mounting experience of suffocating congestion to a moment of total release which is also a moment of vision. Throughout the book the congestion, the com- pression, the helpless anxiety grow. "His heart and his head were congested with anger." "My head feels so tight I don't know what I'm doing," "I'm so choked up and congested anyway I can't see straight," "I feel too choked and strangled," "You've got to let me breathe,"[7] and so on, and when he wants to demonstrate to his father what his estranged wife is doing to him he actually starts to choke himself. It is a graphic enact- ment of a character suffering from the hands of "the world's business" gripped around his throat. To bring this character to some valid moment of transcending vision is the impressive achievement of the book, but to appreciate that achievement we should look first more closely at the character of Tommy Wilhelm.

As we see him at the start he is a representative sort of failure: ex-actor, unemployed, going to seed, eating too much, relying on pills, trying to keep up appearances and defend himself against the world with his cigar and hat (the props of confidence and success), but aware that his meaningless routine is "breaking up," that he has "no position," and that "a huge trouble long presaged but till now formless was due."[8] He has arrived at the point where self-deception and masquerade can no longer be sustained. "Oh, this was a day of reckoning. It was a day, he thought, on which, willing or not, he would take a good close look at the truth."[9] The book follows Tommy having his close look at the truth. He goes over his past life, realising that he was ambitious, sought distinction, and had tried to free himself from "the anxious and narrow life of the average." He had been "eager for life to start." Yet each step, his attempt to get in films, his marriage, was a wrong step, often taken against the warnings of his deeper self. His energy has never been significantly employed. The dubious Dr Tamkin tells him that there are two main souls "the real soul and a pretender soul. Now! Every man realizes that he has to love something or somebody. He feels that he must go outward."[10] Tommy feels the truth of this and wonders where his real soul is. He knows also that "a man is only as good as what he loves,"[11] and he wonders what a man should love since he knows it must not be money. He wants to know what the self is, and what it should love. What makes Tommy a central Bellow figure is that, despite his very real and immobilising, demoralising money problems, he is a "visionary sort of animal. Who has to believe that he can know why he exists. Though he has never seriously tried to find out

why."[12] He is a real victim of the heavy world which
money has created; but he is not a total victim because
even in his last extremity when he is almost a wreck, an
unkempt slob in his father's eyes, he holds on to his intimation that this money world is not the final reality,
that the soul's business must be different from the world's
business even when the latter can be neither resisted nor
denied.

Society has tried to "type" Tommy very much as
Maurice Venice "types" him for certain parts in films;
he has been amenable to such "typing," and the result
has been falsity and ruin. But he has discovered in himself a need to know his real self which is at least the
beginning of salvation. Now because Tommy has this
interest and need to know, he exposes himself to yet
another, subtler form of manipulation and exploitation.
"I guess I am a sucker for people who talk about the
deeper things of life,"[13] he thinks. Exploitation in the
guise of philosophy and advice; the hypnotic power
play of verbal tyrants. For in a world of universal
semi-literacy the theoreticians and word-mongers might
prove to be the most sinister force of all, particularly
when they use or abuse their jumbled ideas and highly-
charged, corrupt rhetoric for base ends. For power,
for money—which is for death. Bellow himself wrote:
"The age is full of great and dangerous monologists.
He-whose-voice-is-heard is the dictator, demagogue,
leader; he-who-makes-us-listen on the public address
system or on the radio and whose monologue leads all
others. The man who can make others listen is the man
who has attained power."[14] And Bellow of course has
always been fascinated by talkers, whether they are
philosophers or confidence tricksters, all who assert
the self through words. Not just in fiction either: for
instance, he interviewed Yellow Kid Weil, a great
Chicago confidence man who made eight million

dollars illicitly and lost it on honest schemes, and was obviously fascinated by the man's ability, his resourcefulness and energy and imagination. He admired his genius for role-playing, for self-projection, for sheer vitality and inventiveness. And he quoted Yellow Kid as saying: "How was I to live? My power lay in words. In words I became a commander."[15] In a world of greedy people perhaps the confidence man deserves to be king. He is a sort of artist—as Thomas Mann showed in *Felix Krull*—even if he is a corrupt parody of real dedicated imagination and talent. He is perhaps a symptom of a sick society which can lead men to deploy all their energy and wit to the getting of money, and in which words are used more for deception than dialogue.

Bellow is aware of the attraction as well as the danger of the word-spinner and it helped him to create one of his most interesting characters—Dr Tamkin, the brilliant pseudo-philosopher who tricks Tommy out of his last seven hundred dollars, bedevilling him with a farrago of ideas, working on him with fantastic stories, sudden insights, and philosophic notions which vary from the plausible to the profound. Sometimes, indeed, he sounds positively Emersonian: *e.g.* "only the present is real—the here-and-now. Seize the day."[16] His ideas penetrate and permeate Tommy. He does not want to give in to destruction and pessimism, he does want to assert something positive about the present, he does want to live in a true sense. Yet how does a man seize the day in contemporary New York? For all his fine phrases Tamkin ends up by seizing only money. What is the true way to celebrate the here-and-now? Tommy feels deeply alienated from New York, as he stresses time and again; it is violent (he finds his mother's grave violated), heavy and hot, ugly and utterly overbearing. Bellow nowhere makes us more vividly aware of the sheer material pressure, the human density, the exhausting physical experience of life in New York. And for Tommy there is no way out. Tamkin's chatter, deceptive yet probing, helps to goad him along to the point of truth, but the lessons Tommy learns are nothing so glib as Tamkin's updated Emersonianism ("self-reliance" is not so easy in modern New York). For him there is no flight, nor any easy solutions. We leave him with his financial problems still unsolved, weeping over the body of an unknown man at a strange funeral.

We cannot say, as some critics do say, that he has learned to seize the day; one could as well suggest that he has succumbed to it. But something at a deep creatural level has been learned and out of the mess of the pretender-Tommy we can discern a new emergent disposition, connected with the real self and a level of reality not reached by the money-world. What Tommy learns is intimately connected with misery, sorrow, and death. Early in the book a line from "Lycidas" drifts back to him along with this line from Shakespeare's sonnets—"love that well which thou must leave ere long."[17] Later comes another scrap of poetry about sorrow—"now of all the world I love thee best"—[18] and by the end of the book he is "helplessly captive to misery."[19] His mounting sadness is complicated by the congestion and suffocation he also feels, until the end is a necessary physical release of tensions and emotions which can no longer be contained, as well as being a vast inarticulate elegy for an anonymous reminder of our common mortality. Wilhelm is actually chasing Tamkin when he is pushed by the crowd into the funeral parlour. But the image of the dead man arrests him. Tommy, harassed by a maximum of the distractions of modern life confronts the state in which man is beyond all distractions.

Soon he was past words, past reason, coherence. He could not stop. The source of all tears had suddenly sprung open within him, black, deep, and hot, and they were pouring out and convulsed his body. . . . The great knot of ill and grief in his throat swelled upward and he gave in utterly and held his face and wept. He cried with all his heart. . . . The flowers and lights fused ecstatically in Wilhelm's blind, wet eyes; the heavy sea-like music came up to his ears. It poured into him where he had hidden himself in the centre of a crowd by the great and happy oblivion of tears. He heard it and sunk deeper than sorrow, through torn sobs and cries toward the consummation of his heart's ultimate need.[20]

Thus the book ends. It is blurred, deeply emotional beyond clear exactness of statement, yet the release is felt and powerfully communicated. What is he weeping for? Many things coalesce in his tears. The dead man is a reminder of the inevitable death of the self, at the same time he is a very specific omen to Tommy, helpless and friendless on this day of reckoning. Tommy's tears are both for humanity and for himself. Yet they also reveal an awareness of the supreme value of life, sheer life itself, existence beyond the assessment of financial success or failure. Succumbing to his tears Tommy at the same time seems to be surmounting his troubles if only because they seem trivial and unreal beside the great central fact of being and non-being which he is now confronting in its full nakedness. In one sense the relief may be temporary—there will still be bills to pay when he leaves the funeral parlour; but having been touched and awed by the great realities of life and death, Tommy will never again be quite such a victim of the world's business. "Love that well which thou must leave ere long." In weeping for his own death Tommy, in a way,

is making a gesture of love towards life. He wants to
live. Money and its attendant pernicious influences have
not killed his heart. But this is not an unprepared
gesture. Earlier in the book when he is thinking about
how alienated people seem from each other he decides
there must be "a larger body, and from this you cannot
be separated."[21] Thus Tommy himself once experienced
a "blaze of love" in an underground corridor for all
the unknown, disfigured outcasts of the world. "And in
the dark tunnel, in the haste, heat, and darkness which
disfigure and make freaks and fragments of nose and
eyes and teeth, all of a sudden, unsought, a general love
for all these imperfect and lurid-looking people burst
out in Wilhelm's breast. He loved them. One and all,
he passionately loved them. They were his brothers
and sisters."[22] Of course the feeling faded away as the
day's worries returned to him. But still he feels that
"that's the right clue and may do me most good.
Something very big. Truth, like."[23]

But more important than this general love is Tommy's
changing attitude towards the burdens of life. Much
of the book revolves around who carries whom. Tommy,
like other Bellow characters, would like to be free, to
cast off impositions and determinism. His early attempts
to get into the films under a new name were a "bid
for liberty." But gradually he has been forced to return
to his "inescapable self." And this self carries a weight.
"The spirit, the peculiar burden of his existence lay
upon him like an accretion, a load, a lump. In any
moment of quiet, when sheer fatigue prevented him
from struggling, he was apt to feel this mysterious
weight, this growth or collection of nameless things
which it was the business of his life to carry about. That
must be what a man was for."[24] So Tommy comes to
the realisation that he "was assigned to be the carrier
of a load which was his own self, his characteristic

self."[25] He moves towards an acquiescence with his fate, an acceptance of his life, which is not a spineless capitulation to it. Tommy makes an act of self-definition by taking up a positive attitude towards his mistakes and all that life has done to him. He affirms the value of life and love just when the forces around him have brought him to the ground. This is one way, perhaps the major one, in which a man can transcend determinism without escaping from it.

Some critics wondered whether Bellow had quite justified his ending. Hassan wondered if "the particular mode of his illumination does not seem rather gratuitous, rather foreign to the concerns he has most steadily expressed throughout the action."[26] While Kazin wrote: "I was troubled by the excessive awareness of the submission, by the lack of someone big enough to fight with life."[27] Richard Chase, on the other hand, who, like other critics, rated the book as Bellow's best so far, said: "only in *Seize the Day* is there a fully adequate, dramatically concentrated image of what the central figure is up against,"[28] and we have noted how much more convincingly solid and undismissible are the obstacles of the world for Tommy than they were for Augie. The book, with its authentic density, its real pain and genuine shouldering of problems, earns its lyric moment, though that moment with all its emotional vagueness is neither a solution nor a resolution of the problems posed by the book. Tommy learned something important about following his real, as opposed to his pretender, self; he learned more than Augie did about the carrying of burdens—yet his reconciliation to the world of others is not fully worked out, nor is his pursuit of the real self followed up. There is nothing false about the book, but there is perhaps something unfinished. The old problem of the conflict between selflessness and selfhood, the outward move toward others and a circling preoccupation with the self—this is opened up but not seen through. But the power and honesty of the book are undeniable and Tommy's crucial discovery is firm and fully earned—namely that the business of life and the world's business are very different, may even be mutually hostile. Yet they are not easily disentangled and there can be no simple flight from one to the other.

REFERENCES

(Page references to *S.T.D.* refer only to the English edition.)

1. *S.T.D.*, p. 50.
2. These three stories were not published in the English edn. of *S.T.D.* so I am citing the original places of publication, *New Yorker*, 5 Feb. 1955.
3. *Commentary*, Mar. 1951.
4. *Discovery*, No. 4, 1956.
5. *S.T.D.*, p. 67.
6. *S.T.D.*, p. 25.
7. *S.T.D.*, pp. 42, 69, 72, 102, 154.
8. *S.T.D.*, p. 9.
9. *S.T.D.*, p. 130.
10. *S.T.D.*, p. 95.
11. *S.T.D.*, p. 16.
12. *S.T.D.*, p. 54.
13. *S.T.D.*, p. 93.
14. "Gide as Writer and Autobiographer," 1951.
15. "A Talk with the Yellow Kid," 1956.
16. *S.T.D.*, p. 90.
17. *S.T.D.*, p. 19.
18. *S.T.D.*, p. 122.
19. *S.T.D.*, p. 149.
20. *S.T.D.*, pp. 159-60.
21. *S.T.D.*, pp. 113-14.
22. *S.T.D.*, p. 114.
23. *S.T.D.*, p. 115.
24. *S.T.D.*, pp. 53-4.
25. *S.T.D.*, p. 54.
26. Ihab Hassan, *Radical Innocence*, 1961.
27. Alfred Kazin, *Contemporaries*, 1962.
28. "The Adventures of Augie March," in *Commentary*, Apr. 1959.

CHAPTER VI

THE FIGHTING LAZARUS

A crowd of facts came upon me with accompanying pressure in the chest. Who—who was I? A millionaire wanderer and wayfarer. A brutal and violent man driven into the world. A man who fled his own country, settled by his forefathers. A fellow whose heart said, *I want, I want*. Who played the violin in despair, seeking the voice of angels. Who had to burst the spirit's sleep, or else.[1]

In his next book Bellow created a character directly opposed to Wilhelm; a character liberated from the constrictions of money and society, who moves outside the pressing determinisms which brought Wilhelm so low. A character big enough and free enough to confront man as pure spirit and evolutionary potential instead of man as victim of social forces. After realism, Bellow turned to romance. When *Henderson the Rain King* appeared in 1959, the critics excelled themselves in providing a rich and varied genealogy for the massive protagonist. One critic, biding his time, pointed out that Henderson had been immediately compared to Don Quixote (twice), Tarzan (twice), Gulliver, Everyman, Huck Finn, Daniel, a Connecticut Yankee (twice), Odysseus, and Captain Ahab. His conclusion was that this was "one of those books clearly constructed for the delight and despair of meaning-hunters." He asked, quite frankly, "What is the story *really* about," and made a pertinent observation. "What is involved here, I think, is the nature and extent of Bellow's commitment to his story."[2] We will return to this point at the end of

the chapter when we discuss the dominant tone and
prevailing atmosphere of the book. But first let us take
stock of the titanic and turbulent Henderson—his
character, his yearnings, his quest and discoveries.
Then we may be able to suggest why Bellow shifted
his attention from the typical Jewish protagonist of his
earlier work, hampered and harassed by a dense urban
environment, and conjured up this violent and bemused
aristocratic giant, with his limitless money, outrageous
strength, his broken teeth, and his insatiable, inarticulate longings. We may also be nearer to understanding
why so many of the ideas which Bellow developed in
his earlier work now appear in a new light, so that
profound notions seem to flirt with their own parodies
and a genuine seriousness of inquiry is jostled and tripped
by the immense comic gusto which hurtles the book
along.

At the start we see mainly a man of "mad habits"—
drinking, chaotically involved with women, raising
pigs in the ancestral home, fighting with an old violin,
flailing around with his inordinate strength, and shouting
out at life in a voice loud enough to bring sudden death
to an old servant. His great tradition cannot provide
him with a function, a satisfying role, a mode of self
realisation. His violence is really a form of immense
brooding frustration. He feels a vague need for some
discipline and he cherishes an intermittent aspiration
to be a doctor; but he feels "displaced," has no sense
of station, and feels the need to find out some basic
truths about the self and its destiny before he can make
terms with society. For, like most Bellow characters,
and indeed many American heroes, he does not know
how to relate himself to other people. "Society is what
beats me. Alone I can be pretty good, but let me go
among people and there's the devil to pay."[3] He is too
rich and too strong to submit to society's net, and he is

in a position to disregard all man-made determinisms until he has identified and satisfied the fermenting energies which goad him into habits and gestures of wild disorder and finally drive him out to Africa in a quest for "essentials." He is rash, unlucky, given more to impulsive action than reflexion—but still amenable to instruction, still flexible; protean but eager for a defining shape. He is the quintessence of ignorant, questing, well-intentioned individualism, 'an exceptional amalgam of vehement forces.'[4] His prime need is to release that vehemence and waken to reality. "I know what it is to lie buried in yourself."[5] All of which qualifies him as a member of that rare class of people that Dahfu characterises as "the fighting Lazaruses."[6]

We shall understand his yearnings better if we examine his motives in making the trip to Africa. Mainly it is a couple of rooms. One, his own. It is insulated, carpeted, so "swept and garnished," and so thoroughly defended from the elements that inside it he feels he is turning into a mere "trophy"[7] with his essential manhood ebbing away. The second belongs to his daily-help who dies so suddenly. Inspecting her rooms Henderson finds the accumulated junk of ages. It reminds him of the grave.

And I thought, Oh, shame, shame! Oh, crying shame! How can we? Why do we allow ourselves? What are we doing? The last little room of dirt is waiting. Without windows. So for God's sake, make a move, Henderson, put forth effort. You, too, will die of this pestilence. Death will annihilate you and nothing will remain, and there will be nothing left but junk.[8]

The encroaching, suffocating litter and rubble of a life lived badly, lived pointlessly, oppresses Henderson to the point where he has to make a colossal effort of disburdenment, mentally and physically. Dahfu says

that Henderson left America "because of a privation
of high conduct."9 Certainly, when drunk he roars out
"There is a curse on this land!"10

His inner voice, which will not be silenced, reiterates
endlessly—"I want," an extreme manifestation of that
"boundless desire," that longing without focus which
Bellow has described as particularly American. And
what Henderson wants, as he gasps or bellows his needs,
turns into a sort of anthology not only of all the desires
of the other characters in Bellow's work, but of the vast
range of romantic and post-romantic aspirations in
general. Seething with desire, vigour, and need Henderson becomes the voice of some basic force and urge.
Almost, one might say, he acts out in something between
pantomime and allegory, a whole chapter in the history
of Western sensibility. He is a semi-burlesque synthesis
of the great questing, exploring, yearning aspirants of
the Western imagination—Ahab crossed with Tarzan
(with perhaps an admixture of Ernest Hemingway,
as Leslie Fiedler has suggested). The critics were right
in detecting a multiple genealogy! He cannot stand unreality, he feels he has to "carry his life to a certain
depth."11 More generally, he yearns to move on from
Becoming to *Being*. "Enough! Time to have Become.
Time to be! Burst the spirit's sleep."12

But if Henderson is a figure of unflagging aspiration,
he is also a victim of frequent humiliation. He exhibits
a tremendous positive, thrusting, "lifting" power (a
power that Bellow admired in Dreiser, and vividly
dramatised by the powerful embrace with which Henderson raises the goddess Mummah); but he is also liable
to be denuded, degraded, and dragged down into the
dust—whether by the army doctors who strip and shave
him, or the Amazons who rip off his clothes and tumble
him into the mud during the rain ritual. Built to wrestle
with gods, Henderson is still humanly vulnerable. He

touches the extremes of our condition—a giant in his hope, a child in his fallibility. Looking back over his adventures he sounds two different notes in his retrospective musing during his letter to his wife. He can say that he has been "called from nonexistence into existence" and describe his ambition in these terms: "to raise my spirit from the earth, to leave the body of this death. I was very stubborn. I wanted to raise myself into another world. My life and deeds were a prison."[13] But despite his gigantic efforts of crashing out, and breaking clear, and moving up he never attains the serene plateau of pure Being. The human lot is perhaps something less perfect and more complicated. Perhaps it is the essence of human desires to be unfulfillable.

I don't think the struggles of desire can ever be won. Ages of longing and willing, willing and longing, and how have they ended? In a draw, dust and dust.[14]

Yet for Henderson there has been a quest, an ordeal, a learning, and the ending does hint at a form of acquiescence and reconciliation which could not have been achieved in any other way. We must now consider the various stages in Henderson's education; an education which provides a bizarre and barbaric complement to that most famous of all American educations—that of Henry Adams. Who was also a traveller, a seeker after wisdom, a man with a "service ideal" which he could never put into practice. And also an intimate of Henderson's more respectable ancestors.

"Untrammel me. Heavenly Father, open up my dumb heart and for Christ's sake preserve me from unreal things."[15] Such is the prayer that arises spontaneously in Henderson's troubled being. And he knows that truth and reality will not be come by easily. Chopping wood, he gets hit by a chunk of it and speculates that truth comes "in blows."[16] And from then on his life becomes harsher, more rigorous until he approaches shudderingly close to the deep ultimate secrets of savagery and annihilation. First comes the decampment from civilisation—the preliminary act of untrammeling, as it were. Henderson plants himself in Africa "the ancient bed of mankind."[17] Once there he has to abandon himself to whatever Africa brings to him—making errors, taking blows, submitting to strange embraces, grazing death itself. From the time of his fight with Prince Itelo—half sport, half ceremony —all civilised standards of behaviour are left behind. And it is that time which Henderson defines as "the hour which burst my spirit's sleep."[18]

The first tribe he encounters—the Arnewi—are gentle, peaceful, kindly, abstaining from all violence and respecting their animals as their friends. They seem to exist in a state of continual poetry and placid enchantment. The old Queen Willattale is the very incarnation of stability: she seems to be effortlessly sustained by the rhythms of life itself. Touching her breast for greeting—and Henderson has to touch many things in Africa including lions and corpses—it feels "as if I were touching the secrets of life."[19] He expects to hear the answer to the ultimate mystery of things from her, but of course it is not to be come by so easily. Henderson envies her great, benign, unprotesting calm but he is far, yet, from being able to emulate it. All she can tell him is "Grun-tu-molani. Man want to live."[20] Henderson is exhilarated by this pithy summary of his deepest need, and by way of gratitude he endeavours to clear the village cistern of its plague of frogs. This bit of "Connecticut Yankee" technological horse-play ends disastrously with Henderson blowing up the cistern along with the frogs. He is too much the restless, over-dynamic interferer to be able to reside with the Arnewi. Disgraced and humiliated he returns to the desert to embark on the second and harder stage of his education.

The Wariri are "chillen dahkness" as Romilayu, the guide, puts it. They greet Henderson with an ambush, put him in a cell with a corpse for the first night, and offer no hospitality. He notices people drinking, quarrelling, and abusing each other. Some of the men wear human jaw bones. On his way to the palace Henderson passes bodies hanging from a scaffold and just before his first interview with the king he hears "the roar of a wild beast." The King, Dahfu, is the most important of all Henderson's guides and tutelary presences. He is utterly calm and yet he seems to gleam with some unusual intensity of life. As soon as he sees him, Henderson has "the conviction that we could approach ultimates together."[21] He feels, by contrast with the King's soaring serenity, that he is "all limit-ation . . . contracted and cramped."[22] From this King he hopes to learn the secret of Being. He shows himself an apt pupil by his impulsive participation in the rain ceremony: at last he has found a task commensurate with his unruly, unused strength, and by lifting the god-dess, by immersing himself in the cruelty and violence and unconcealed ferocity of the ceremony, he shows himself ready for further instruction in some of the more rudimentary truths and some of the more amazing potentialities of humanity. Himself a bringer of chaos, Henderson learns "what savagery can be," and every-thing that happens to him with this tribe brings him nearer to a proper confrontation of what he calls "the biggest problem"—the encounter with death.

To summarise all Dahfu's ideas would be to miss the point. He is himself an equivocal figure—a potential redeemer of mankind but not without a hint of Faustian over-reaching. Henderson occasionally loses confidence in him and feels that his brilliance is insecure, resting "on doubtful underpinnings." His ideas often threaten to topple over into absurdity, or vanish into incomprehensibility. Yet it is from those who venture far out that man learns most, and Henderson certainly comes to a clearer understanding of his main problem with the help of Dahfu, the problem being a basic one in Bellow's work—how should a man properly *submit* to reality and at the same time how can he attempt to *transcend* himself and slough off hampering limitations. Just as the seed submits to the desert yet ends by emerging as a flower. Dahfu gives Henderson lessons in submission and transcendence. For as he points out: "Granted grun-tu-molani is much, but it is not alone sufficient."[23]

Submission Henderson learns by going down, literally, into the lion's den. Dahfu himself is clearly sustained and nourished by his periodic contact with the lion he has caught and tamed; and Henderson feels that the King is conducting his experiment for the benefit of "mankind as a whole, which is tired of itself and needs a shot in the arm from animal nature."[24] (It is worth mentioning that Bellow was, at this time, influenced by the ideas of Wilhelm Reich, who has similar notions of re-discovering the real animal self.) Dahfu persuades Henderson to approach closer and closer to the lion, finally telling him to drop down on all fours and release himself in roaring and running. The purpose of this lesson with the lion is clear. The lion is "unavoidable": Henderson has spent his life in "momentous avoidances." "You fled what you were. You did not believe you had to perish."[25] Now if he will really confront the lion and all it represents—"She will make consciousness to shine. She will burnish you. She will force the present moment upon you."[26] Henderson at first resists the encounter, he is "contracted and self-recoiled," he is too conscious, and consciousness, says the King, isolates the self. Whereas if a man can relax he will pass through fear into a new beauty, with all unhealthy "ego-emphasis" removed. This is the lion's lesson: she "does not take issue with the inherent."[27] Henderson, in consenting to relapse into the beast, being brought down, as he says, to "the bottom of things," learns something of the deep flexibility and positive peace which comes from abandoning the fears and anxieties, the longings and the loneliness, which result from an excess of consciousness. But something refuses to sink back into this animal state—"my human longing." And it is this ineradicable human aspiration which prompts Dahfu to his most passionate ideas. He knows the need to descend to the lion; but he comprehends the longing "to rise to summits."

He starts from this basic idea: the world of facts is "real and not to be altered," "But then there is the noumenal department, and there we create and create and create."[28] Man is "a master of imagination." "Imagination is a force of nature. . . . It converts to actual. It sustains, it alters, it redeems!"[29] Dahfu believes "in the transformation of human material": man is "the artist of suggestions,"[30] he creates himself according to his conception of himself. Tragically, the human imagination has all too often created monsters; but what types of beauty and goodness and nobility the right sort of imagination could create! This is the crux of the other half of Dahfu's instruction—"For the noble self-conception is everything."[31] And it is because Dahfu refuses to be pessimistic about human possibilities, because he has faith that "the noble will have its turn in the world,"[32] that Henderson feels so exhilarated and uplifted by him. Mankind is locked in a meaningless cycle of "fearing and desiring." Henderson himself feels exhausted from being ridden by these alternating forces. He agrees with Dahfu: "Any good man will try to break the cycle."[33] It must be possible to conceive a superior type of human being. But of course Henderson can get no further than this. Salvation may lie in the creative imagination, but salvation has yet to come. Dahfu is killed in a lion hunt and when Henderson stares down at a real wild lion, not a tame one, he realises that there is a principle of horror and death in reality which hitherto he had not been aware of. Effectively this means that his instruction ends with nothing settled. Reality turns out to be a more ferocious, alien thing than he had realised; while the effort to break out of the cycle of endless Becoming seems doomed to remain the dream of the advanced imagination. It would be inhuman to return to a real lion wildness: it is, as well, impossible to scale those summits. So, with a timely escape from the tribe and a definite decision to enter medical school, Henderson's African education comes to an end. He has no new solutions perhaps, but he does have some convictions. Nobility is not unreal and human greatness is no illusion. Much of his ranting, insatiable egotism has fallen from him and at least his life promises to exhibit both more peace and more purpose. One forgets the unresolved issues of the book in the invigorating beauty of the last scene, with Henderson holding the young Persian boy and once more in-dulging his love of movement—"leaping, leaping, pounding, and tingling over the pure white lining of the gray Arctic."[34]

Many critics felt that the ending was a disappoint-ment, an evasion. "We never see Henderson back in the United States . . . his transformation is finally no more than a matter of assertion on his part."[35] Or again:

the note of affirmation on which Mr. Bellow closes is not in the least convincing, and altogether lacks the force to counteract the magnificent passages of anguish and despair that fill the body of the book.[36]

Fiedler thought that the euphoria of the book was "un-earned." I think there is some justice in these charges but the basic drive and effort of the book is sincere and convincing. It is not a matter of answers, or desperate euphoric exclamations, or fits of hysterical yea-saying. Take two of Henderson's most intense reactions. In front of the octopus in the aquarium when he feels "a cosmic coldness" and senses that "Death is giving me notice":[37] and then when he wakes up in Africa one morning overwhelmed by the beauty of the sunlight on a wall, he feels "some powerful magnificence not human." The "vital experience" it gives him is like "the fringe of Nirvana" and without such moments, when he feels flooded by the possible poetry of existence, Henderson feels he would simply be condemned to die "a slave to low-grade fear and turbulence."[38] Henderson wants to discover and proclaim the positive potentialities of life before death robs him, and us, of all chance to experience them. "Humankind has to sway itself more intentionally toward beauty."[39] And nobility. This is the gesture the book makes, and if nothing else, it communicates its sense of need and resolution. What I think *is* merely asserted is the supreme importance of "love." "Whatever gains I ever made were always due to love and nothing else."[40] His relationship with his wife is an amiable burlesque, and, indeed, despite his impulsive admirations and affections, it is hard to see Henderson ever having real relationships with any one. What one does feel is that he will never really surmount or transform his ebullient and tormented individualism.

But if we think for a moment of Henderson not as a single individual character but as the very incarnation of individualism, it is possible to see the book in a different light. It has not escaped the notice of critics that the book contains many Nietzschian ideas.[41] *Thus*

Spake Zarathustra provides many anticipatory echoes, *e.g.*, "Therefore, O my brethren, it needeth a *new nobility* opposed to the rabble and to all tyrannies, to write anew on new tables the word 'noble'," and "Man is a thing to be surmounted."[42] The parallel seems even closer when we recall that Henderson is constantly "embroiled with animals"—the pigs he keeps, the frogs he blows up, the lion he learns to run with, the old bear he once embraced (as they travelled on the roller-coaster together in a fairground), not to mention the octopus that frightens him, the cat he tries to shoot, the crabs he suffered from in the army. He often recalls the prophecy of Daniel: "They shall drive you from among men, and thy dwelling shall be with the beasts of the field." All this intimate involvement with the lower forms of natural life is clearly part of his education, his resurrection into reality. All the more interesting, therefore, to find that Zarathustra's first discourse concerns the "three metamorphoses of the spirit," into a camel, a lion, and a child. Now of course there is no exact copying or even a direct parallel: but there are hints and clues that Bellow has included some deliberate echoes of Nietzsche's work. Thus one of the tasks of the "burden-bearing" spirit is "to enter foul waters, if these be the waters of truth, and not to repulse the chilly frogs and hot toads therein"; and again the lion is unable "to create new values," but he can "create for himself freedom for new creation," which is very like what Dahfu was trying to teach Henderson down in the lion pit. Nietzsche then says the lion must become a child, for whereas the lion can only say "nay" to false duties and restrictions, the child is "an holy yea-saying."[43] Henderson is a kind of child and his last act of qualified affirmation is achieved by literally embracing a child—the last of many strange and influential embraces in his travels. This is clearly not mere borrowing on Bellow's part. Could he, perhaps, be writing a weird, fantastic allegory of Nietzschian man; for it was, after all, that writer who asserted the supreme value of the individual as "superman" to a point where few have followed him? Perhaps that is going too far, but Bellow himself has referred to the book as being about "the comedy of self-concern," and this certainly gives us the clue that we are not to take Henderson wholly seriously.

For after all he is a tremendously egotistical, presumptious buffoon; what with his insistence on the supreme importance of the history of his teeth, his inordinate petulance expressed with a near ridiculous grandiloquence ("If I couldn't have my soul it would cost the earth a catastrophe"), his incipient solipsism ("Reality is *you*," he says, looking in a mirror), his fondness for his own suffering, and the inflated, overweening, self-dramatising romanticism which pervades his rhetoric. In an essay, Bellow discusses at some length the changing attitudes which have been taken by various writers to "romantic individualism" since it "began to appear fraudulent." In the work of writers like Svevo, he says, "deeply subjective self-concern is ridiculed." He goes on to say that some writers are now exploiting "comically the romantic theme of the precious, unique self," and this takes him to a favourite talking point:

> a small handful of writers . . . have offered us, in comedy, our only relief from the long prevalent mood of pessimism, discouragement, and low-seriousness. . . . Let us hope that, superfluity and solemn nonsense having been laughed and hooted away by the comic spirit, we may see the return of a genuine moral seriousness in literature.

He then goes on to say that whatever we decide "about

the meaning of an individual life," there are now "more individual lives than ever" and that we need comedy to oppose "the popular orgy of wretchedness in modern literature."[44] Clearly *Henderson* was his own comic contribution to this cause. But the big question remains, and I cannot see that Bellow has answered it either in the essay or in the book. What value does *he* attribute to the self, the individual life? If Henderson is absurd in his self-preoccupation, then just how absurd is he? Clearly Bellow is not in sympathy with those modern writers like Hofmannsthal who affirm that "Individuality is an arabesque we have discarded." But his work is increasingly marked by an equivocal awareness both of the dangers and absurdity of excessive self-concern.

That is why the critic was justified in asking just how much was Bellow committed to his story. Is it an allegory, a parody, a romance, a fantasy? Bellow himself has written an article warning people against "deep reading":

> Novels are being published today which consist entirely of abstractions, meanings, and while our need for meanings is certainly great, our need for concreteness, for particulars is even greater. We need to see how human beings act after they have appropriated or assimilated the meanings. Meanings themselves are a dime a dozen.[45]

Fairly said: yet where does that leave Henderson's quest which is so persistent in the pursuit of meaning, and so relatively free from all concrete obstructions? Is it, perhaps, all a dream, an escape from American mess into African reverie; is it a psychological journey into the continent of the self? (As Sir Thomas Browne said, "There is all Africa and her prodigies in us.") He does say that "every guy has his own Africa"[46] which can be taken in a number of ways. And despite the great brilliance of many of the descriptions of Africa —scorchingly authentic, some of them—there remains a residual feeling of mirage, of dream. "For me the entire experience has been similar to a dream."[47] Should we take that as the crucial hint? Yet so many of Bellow's chief preoccupations are tussled with and thrashed out in the book that it is difficult to believe that he wants them to be laughed away as the self-induced fantasy of a titanic child who is half superman and half clown. Perhaps the surface of the book is comic and the centre is deeply serious; perhaps Henderson is extravagant to the point of absurdity, yet his need and yearning are real and important. It could be that Bellow has put his ideas into a comic perspective to see how they will survive the test.

The book remains, I think, somewhat enigmatic, its over-all intention unclear, its perspective shifting, its level of seriousness always in question. It manifests, indeed enacts, a compelling joy derived from the sheer fact of human consciousness; but it is uncertain to the point of hysteria on the question of individual value. Henderson's voice can be urgent and involving, and then again it can lapse into a sort of glib vernacular bravado which trivialises the main issues. Yet when the book reaches away from negation towards celebration; when we feel the full force of Bellow's refusal to accept despair, then it takes hold of us in a positive way beyond the scope of mere parody. Something important, we feel, is brewing up even if we cannot quite identify it through the tangled exuberance of the novel's surface. Henderson is a kind of fool, but persistent enough in his folly to reach the threshold of wisdom, and when he struggles to grasp and hold the notion of a new nobility attainable by men, then, whether he is waking or sleeping, comic or profound, we listen to him; and listening we suddenly seem to glimpse what it might mean to burst the spirit's sleep. Such glimpses are the reward of the novel.

REFERENCES

1. *H.R.K.*, p. 76.
2. Reed Whittlemore "Safari among the Wariri," in *New Republic*, 16 Mar. 1959.
3. *H.R.K.*, p. 49.
4. *H.R.K.*, p. 271.
5. *H.R.K.*, p. 277.
6. *H.R.K.*, p. 217.
7. *H.R.K.*, p. 24.
8. *H.R.K.*, p. 40.
9. *H.R.K.*, p. 264.
10. *H.R.K.*, p. 38.
11. *H.R.K.*, p. 105.
12. *H.R.K.*, p. 160.
13. *H.R.K.*, p. 284.
14. *H.R.K.*, p. 285.
15. *H.R.K.*, p. 253.
16. *H.R.K.*, p. 23.
17. *H.R.K.*, p. 42.
18. *H.R.K.*, p. 67.
19. *H.R.K.*, p. 72.
20. *H.R.K.*, p. 85.
21. *H.R.K.*, p. 156.
22. *H.R.K.*, p. 160.
23. *H.R.K.*, p. 218.
24. *H.R.K.*, p. 251.
25. *H.R.K.*, p. 260.
26. *Ibid.*
27. *H.R.K.*, p. 263.
28. *H.R.K.*, p. 167.
29. *H.R.K.*, p. 271.
30. *H.R.K.*, p. 268.
31. *Ibid.*
32. *H.R.K.*, p. 215.
33. *H.R.K.*, p. 297.
34. *H.R.K.*, p. 341.
35. Dan Jacobson, "The Solitariness of Saul Bellow," 1959.
36. Review of *H.R.K.* by Norman Podhoretz in *New York Herald Tribune Book Review*, 22 Feb. 1959.
37. *H.R.K.*, p. 19.
38. *H.R.K.*, p. 102.
39. *H.R.K.*, p. 282.
40. *H.R.K.*, p. 339.
41. See Marcus Klein, "A Discipline of Nobility," in *Kenyon Review*. XXIV, no. 2. Spring 1962.
42. F. W. Nietzsche, *Thus Spake Zarathustra*, trans. A. Tille, 1933, pp. 181, 29.
43. *H.R.K.*, pp. 19-20.
44. See Saul Bellow, "Literature," Part Three in *The Great Ideas Today*, 1963, pp. 164, 170-1.
45. Saul Bellow, "Deep Readers of the World, Beware!" *New York Times Book Review*, 15 Feb. 1959.
46. *H.R.K.*, p. 275.
47. *H.R.K.*, p. 280.

CHAPTER VII

THE PRISONER OF PERCEPTION

His face was before him in the blotchy mirror. It was bearded with lather. He saw his perplexed, furious eyes and he gave an audible cry. *My God! Who is this creature? It considers itself human. But what is it? Not human of itself. But has the longing to be human.*[1]

This is Moses E. Herzog, the central figure in Bellow's most recent novel, entitled *Herzog*. (His name almost certainly derives from Joyce's *Ulysses* where there is a minor character called Moses Herzog who is a put-upon Jewish merchant. It may also contain a distant reference to the famous and very brave mountaineer, Maurice Herzog.) This book—Bellow's most impressive to this date—seems to summarise and contain all the questions, the problems, the feelings, the plights, and the aspirations worked over in the previous novels, and it follows them out to their extremest reaches. It seems to be the result of a conclusive grappling with the gathering preoccupations of years. Herzog himself is clearly a descendant, if not a summation, of Bellow's other main characters—worried, harassed, brought down, messed up. His private life is at a point of chaos—for he is trying to recover from a disastrous second marriage which has just ended in divorce. He is condemned to perpetual compulsive introspection, the victim of memories which refuse to be shut out, racked by endless, nagging cerebration. He seems terribly isolated and cut-off, wandering the congested city streets, brooding apart in lonely rooms. The book contains few actual incidents in the present—an abortive trip to Vineyard Haven, a night with a girl friend, a visit to Chicago to see one of his children which ends with a car crash, the return to an old tumble-down house in the country which was where his second marriage reached its ultimate crisis. The significant action mainly takes part in his head. People and incidents teem through his memory, precipitating great bouts of agitated soul-searching and pounding speculation. More than that, his mind heaves under the weight and pressure, not only of his personal worries, but of the modern city, the innumerable problems of the modern age; ultimately it finds itself struggling with the deepest questions and mysteries of Man himself. His mind seems compelled to take on itself the burden of the whole world, the problem of mankind; yet as a physical being his relationships are fouled up, he is separated from his children, he is one of the struggling sweating mass—powerless, something of a failure, not a little lost. Yet his mind will not be stilled. There is irony as well as urgency in his predicament and Bellow excels himself in this book by presenting not only the importance, but also the curse and the comedy of intense consciousness. Herzog's is a representative modern mind, swamped with ideas, metaphysics and values, and surrounded by messy facts. It labours to cope with them all. The book enacts that labour.

At first sight, the meaning of the book might seem to be the sum of all the dozens of ideas that course through Herzog's mind. Yet a more careful view reveals a deeper, subtler intent. The book moves from a corrosive restlessness to a point of temporary rest, and the most important meaning is in that actual movement: the internal labour finally gives way to a glimpse of peace. A consideration of the form and technique of the book can help us to understand this better. A brief opening passage shows us a "tranquil" Herzog, alone in his old country house during the "peak of summer." Then it takes us back to the start of all his troubles. "Late in spring Herzog had been overcome by the need to explain, to have it out, to justify, to put in perspective, to clarify, to make amends."[2] This compulsion to *understand*— typical of Bellow's protagonists—manifests itself in Herzog's habit of making endless notes and jottings, recording fragmentary thoughts, and observations. More than that he gets into the habit of writing letters— to friends, relations, dead ancestors, politicians, philosophers, finally even to God. Many of them are unfinished, none of them, as far as we know, are ever sent. Perhaps they are all imaginary, part of his internal continuum, sudden moments of excited hyper-consciousness when the mind engages in silent partnerless dialogues—"having it out," trying to clarify. Meanwhile Herzog is often sitting or lying down, "in the coop of his privacy." For the bulk of the book we are in that coop with him—going over things, witnesses of this endless, silent self-examination. It is not systematic: like his life it is mismanaged and patternless. He cannot organise the mixed swarm of facts, notions and ideas: "consciousness when it doesn't clearly understand what to live for, what to die for, can only abuse and ridicule itself."[3] For much of the book Herzog suffers from "unemployed consciousness."

The book has to bring us not only the excitement of the ideas, but the strain, the futility, the near insanity which Herzog experiences. So the reminiscences and the thoughts and the letters flow, one into the other, like a troubled stream. There are sudden interruptions, extremely vivid, graphic evocations of New York or Chicago—unrelated, sudden heightenings of external pressure. The harsh noise and density of the city seem only to drive Herzog deeper into himself. He is never more lost in thought than on the subway. Significant

B—G

human contact is minimal; even with Ramona, his current girl friend, he seems ultimately detached, only intermittently stimulated to a brief sexual activity accompanied by a little incipient emotion. He can recall many affairs; he loves his brothers and children; he has long talks with certain friends. But for the most part he seems quite incapable of any genuine relationships. His memory is densely populated—yet he moves like a solitary, sealed up in himself, ridden by a million thoughts. Writing letters to the void, while reality ebbs away from him.

But a counter-movement grows increasingly strong —a desire to re-engage simple reality, a yearning for a reprieve from this excess of solitary cerebration, a desire to pass beyond the impossible task of mental justification. His first instinct had been to explain. By the end he is meditating:

> *A curious result of the increase of historical consciousness is that people think explanation is a necessity of survival. They have to explain their condition. And if the unexplained life is not worth living, the explained life is unbearable, too.*[4]

The book follows out his doomed attempts to explain and synthesise until we can feel with Herzog the need and the possibility for some new commencement and calm somewhere on the other side of "explanation." At the end Herzog is tranquil in his country house—as we glimpsed him at the start. Now we understand that tranquillity. But only because we have experienced to the full the turmoil which preceded it.

We shall have to look more closely at some of the ideas that Herzog wrestles with for they are crucial ideas in Bellow's work. But it must first be emphasised that Herzog is in no normal state: it is part of the meaning of the book that these ideas are being turned over by a mind in the throes of a riot of subjectivism. He is often in the state he finds himself enduring in Grand Central Station "both visionary and muddy . . . feverish, damaged, angry, quarrelsome, and shaky."[5] On a train he will start various letters to people as various as Adlai Stevenson, Ramona, Nehru, Commissioner Wilson—and himself. His reaction at the time is typical:

Quickly, quickly, more! . . . Herzog now barely looking through the tinted, immovable, sealed window felt his eager, flying spirit streaming out, speaking, piercing, making clear judgments, uttering final explanations, necessary words only. He was in a whirling ecstasy. He felt at the same time that his judgments exposed the boundless, baseless bossiness and wilfulness, the nagging embodied in his mental constitution.[6]

The sealed window—the soaring mind: the certainty as to the importance of his thoughts—a suspicion that they result from a ridiculous tantrum. That is typical Herzog. He cannot select or filter his thoughts. "I am a prisoner of perception, a compulsory witness."[7] This is a mind with no certainties, no calm programme, no sure focus. A mind in pain. "He wrote to Spinoza. *Thoughts not causally connected were said by you to cause pain. I find that is indeed the case. Random association, when the intellect is passive, is a form of bondage.*"[8]

Like many another alienated observer, he wonders if anguish and detachment are the necessary condition of his calling. "Moses had to see reality. Perhaps he was somewhat spared from it so that he might see it better, not fall asleep in its thick embrace. Awareness was his work; extended consciousness was his line, his business. Vigilance."[9] Looking at his brother, a man immersed in business, Herzog contrasts himself—"a man like me has shown the arbitrary withdrawal of proud subjectivity from the collective and historical progress of mankind."[10] But he says this in self-mockery, and by the end he drops the idea as a vain-glorious falsehood. Gradually, the prisoner starts to emerge. Here is a crucial moment after a heavy spell of speculation and vast generalisations:

> But then he realized that he did not need to perform elaborate abstract intellectual work—work he had always thrown himself into as if it were the struggle for survival. But not thinking is not necessarily fatal. Did I really believe that I would die when thinking stopped?[11]

(Herzog alternates between addressing himself as "I" and "he", and even "you"; while not completely schizophorenic, it does suggest mental disturbance as well as comic detachment.) The habit of subjectivism, explanation, thought itself, becomes almost a plague, a genuine neurosis, of which he is at least partially cured by the end of the book as he moves towards reality's "thick embrace."

But his self-communings and memories compromise the bulk of the book. True, the city-scapes are incomparably vivid, detailed, and pungent; essentially *there* so we can really feel the background against which the modern mind works, and has to work. Herzog feels part of the New York mess, and indeed there seems to be at times an intimate connexion between the city and his thoughts. Perhaps the teeming confusion of its chaos agitates his mind into a state of over-excited emulation—the city triggering off the spasms of unrelated thoughts, just as the thoughts sometimes grind to an inconclusive halt in the congestion of the city streets. Thus in Chicago: "He was perhaps as midwestern and unfocused as these same streets. Not so much determinism, he thought, as lack of determining elements—the absence of a formative power."[12] For all that, the most important reality in the book is inside Herzog's head, in the ramifications of his ungovernable memory and the fretful reachings of his mind. It is there that we meet most of the characters in his life, and relive some of his most intense experiences. It is there that Herzog establishes contact with his ancestors and re-enacts his "ancient times." As though he is trying to form some sort of community in his head to compensate for the absence of it in society at large. It is part of his effort to "make steady progress from disorder to harmony,"[13] to capture a sense of lineage out of the welter of the past —the past of Moses Herzog, of his family, his race, his culture, Man himself. Many of his letters are to the dead. "But then why shouldn't he write the dead? He lived with them as much as with the living—perhaps more."[14] He knows what an "insidious blight" nostalgia is, but his prolonged excursions into the past are only partially self-indulgence and escapism. For it is in his memory that Herzog is seeking some lost reality, some necessary key which will help him to align himself with the norms from which he has wandered and blundered into his personal chaos and separation. He must expose himself to everything, excluding nothing (not even the traumatic sexual assault he suffered as a child) before he can learn true acceptance and a new orientation. Mental regurgitation is part of his therapy: the way back to a point at which life can be resumed lies through memory. "Engrossed, unmoving in his chair, Herzog listened to the dead at their dead quarrels."[15] Some of the most powerful and moving scenes are of his family, his youth, the sufferings of his "late unlucky father": scenes and characters are re-created with an astonishing and compelling wealth of circumstantial detail, while Herzog seems to go into a sort of catatonic trance, engulfed by the past.

Note that Bellow is not concerned to give a straightforward, chronological biography of Herzog. He is

concerned to show a middle-aged confused man beset
by teeming fragments of the past, trying to relate them,
seeking coherence, trying to disentangle from them all
some sense of necessary ancestry, and stabilising orientation. Similarly with the characters and events of
Herzog's own adult life—they are recalled, summoned
up in love or anger, or allowed to drift in and out of
the periphery of his mind . There are well over a score
of characters, who loom into focus with extreme individual vividness—his wives, his women, psychiatrists,
lawyers, fellow academics, brothers, writers, childhood
friends, as well as his parents and older relations.
Inevitably many of the incidents he recalls with these
people are essentially conversations, discussions, dis-
agreements, rows. Apart from sex, and some travel,
most of Herzog's more recent experience has been mainly
verbal. This indeed, is perhaps part of the disease—his
own, his age's. "People legislate continually by means
of talk."[16] Like Augie, Herzog is surrounded by people
who want to give him advice, manipulate him, impose
their view of things, their realities, on his. Some of them
—his second wife, her lover, her lawyer—actually plot
against him for his money, and his children, but most
of the pressures are verbal. Augie found himself surrounded by Machiavellians: Herzog is set down among
"Reality-Instructors"—people who positively enjoy
thrusting forward the low view of truth, cruel in their
relish of the nastiness of life. And even Moses himself
recognises that he, too, wants to teach his ideas. "*A very
special sort of lunatic expects to inculcate his principles.* Sandor
Himmelstein, Valentine Gersbach, Madeleine P. Herzog,
Moses himself. *Reality Instructors. They want to teach you—to
punish you with—the lessons of the Real.*"[17] But one question
abides with Herzog which he silently puts to the world
of Reality-Instructors. "*What makes you think realism
must be brutal?*"[18] Part of his quest is for a higher view

which nevertheless does not blink the brutality which is undoubtedly there.

Herzog recalls people and incidents as often as not because he wishes to take issue with their views, or consider the implications of their acts. We get very little external reality straight—indeed it is possible that the whole book is a reminiscence. (There is a slight, perhaps deliberate ambiguity, about the time lapse between the start and the end. One is not sure whether something is actually taking place or being remembered. Indeed, it is possible that Herzog is remembering previous memories. The book ends where it began.) Situations, characters, and events for the most part come to us coloured by his memory, penetrated by his questioning: often broken up or interrupted by a burst of letter writing. Herzog calls his letter-writing and scribbling of odd notes "ridiculous," but he falls into it continually. Some of the letters are comic, some angry, some desperate, some urgent, many of them theoretical and peda-gogic. They are a way of relieving the accumulating pressures on his mind; also they are part of his vast attempt to take stock, understand, and clarify. Into them he puts his needs, his resentments, his quarrels with the creeds of his age; through them he expresses his inchoate beliefs and tentative faith. Perhaps also they not only help him to come to terms with the dizzying clutter of his life and times, but also serve as a means whereby he can disburden himself of that clutter. But as a phenomenon, irrespective of what Herzog writes in them, these letters and notes are symptoms of a plight and desire which are basic in Bellow's work. Herzog says to himself, in words which remind us of so many other Bellow protagonists: "I seem to have been stirred fiercely by a desire to communicate, or by the curious project of attempted communication."[19] All those prolific letters simply serve to emphasise Herzog's silence, his basic isolation and apartness and indrawnness. He carries the world in his head. But the desire to communicate is real and points the way to a possible redemption from a habit of introspection which could lead to solipsism.

Herzog's thoughts and concerns are too various to summarise; indeed their profuse, unrelated multiplicity is an essential part of the meaning of the book. But a few concerns which have always seriously engaged Bellow recur, and Herzog wrestles with problems and ideas that other characters in Bellow's work have also attacked and pondered, and that Bellow himself has discussed in many articles. Some of these should be mentioned. For instance Herzog returns continually to the question of the value and importance of the individual self. The great work he was meditating before he started to go to pieces was going to show "how life could be lived by renewing universal connections; overturning the last of the Romantic errors about the uniqueness of the Self,"[20] and he thinks back with some irony to the time when as a student he gave an Emersonian address maintaining "The Main enterprise of the world . . . is the upbuilding of a man. The private life of one man shall be a more illustrious monarchy . . . than any kingdom in history."[21] On the other hand he is disgusted by the slick contemporary pessimists who maintain that you must "sacrifice your poor, squawking, niggardly individuality which may be nothing anyway (from an analytic viewpoint) but a persistent infantile megalomania, or (from a Marxian point of view) a stinking little bourgeois property—to historical necessity".[22] Against low sneering realists, Herzog prefers Romanticism. But on the other hand the objections to the cult of selfhood remain. Herzog oscillates continually and decides "perhaps a moratorium on definitions of human nature is now best."[23] But secretly he really resists taking the view which degrades human worth, even though he knows what it is to long to escape from the burden of individuality. Secondly, the problem of freedom worries him: "people can be free now but the freedom doesn't have any content. It's like a howling emptiness."[24] Technology has "created private life but gave nothing to fill it with."[25] What does personal freedom mean; how much are we historically determined? Herzog thinks of Tolstoy's concept of freedom, and would seem to sympathise with it. *"That man is free whose condition is simple, truthful—real. To be free is to be released from historical limitation."*[26] A dignified ideal—yet to step out into the street is to be buffeted by evidence of limitations.

Thirdly, Herzog refuses to believe the modern age is worse than any other and will not endorse pessimism. Spengler's notion of the decline of the West with its implication that the great age for Jews is gone forever, made him sick with rage as a youth: and when he reads that Heidegger talks about "the fall into the quotidian," he writes a letter to him asking *"When did this fall occur? Where were we standing when it happened?"*[27] The potentialities of human life must be perennial. Though there is evil in the world he refuses to concentrate on it as the sole reality. He hears the most appalling evidence of sheer evil in the court room. The description of how a woman, without any tears or remorse, killed her child while her lover lay on the bed, watching and smoking, makes him feel violently sick. It is inexplicable, irremediable evil. "He opened his mouth to relieve the pressure he felt. He was wrung, and wrung again, and wrung again, again."[28] It is this incident which makes him go to Chicago, intending to kill Madeleine and her lover because he has a notion they are mistreating his child. Of course, he has no murder in his heart and transcends his moment of aggressive impulse. His attitude to life is essentially creative not destructive. There is evil but he feels we must look away from it, beyond it. He feels that our age is too fond of regarding itself as monstrous, that an insidious prestige is now attached to "the negative." Vengefully, we deny all possibility of transcendence. The human imagination has been deflected and feeds on murder and death: "*Safe, comfortable people playing at crisis, alienation, apocalypse and desperation, make me sick,*"[29] writes Herzog to a fellow professor. All this is the wrong path for civilisation. "*We love apocalypses too much, and crisis ethics, and florid extremism with its thrilling language. Excuse me, no. I've had all the monstrosity I want.*"[30] To another he writes:

> *Has the filthy moment come when moral feeling dies, conscience disintegrates, and respect for liberty, law, public decency, all the rest collapse in cowardice, decadence, blood? . . . I can't accept this foolish dreariness. We are talking about the whole of mankind.*[31]

He thinks that "*mankind is making it—making it in glory though deafened by the explosions of blood.*" This is not callousness in Herzog; rather it is an insistence not only on the futility but on the dangers of dwelling on evil and death, nourishing the imagination on suffering and despair. Herzog wants to get away from the insidious attractions of nihilism. He is working for a change of heart.

These, then, are some of the ideas that possess Herzog. He is convinced of their importance; he wants to change the world. And Bellow is careful to show that there is some comic presumption in all this along with a fair amount of egotism. Not for nothing is Herzog often caught looking at his own reflexion—he is unusually self-absorbed and self-important. Balance is restored by continual reminders of Herzog as a struggling physical

THE PRISONER OF PERCEPTION 99

creature; and he himself is continually mocking himself,
undercutting his high mental intentions. We catch him
at a transition point, waking to the ludicrous side of
his conviction that "the progress of civilization—indeed,
the survival of civilization—depended on the successes
of Moses E. Herzog."32 He has it in him to want to be a
new law-giver to mankind (as his name suggests) but
his mind has reached a dangerous point when it can
think "If I am right, the problem of the world's coherence, and all responsibility for it, becomes mine."33
Herzog himself comes to smile at himself, mentally
legislating for the whole world while crammed into a
subway car. After all, his own life is a "catalogue of
errors"; he has been self-righteous, conceited in his
suffering, monstrously egotistical, mediocre and merely
"flirting a little with the transcendent." These are rigorous self criticisms; more usually it is the comic futility
of his thinking that strikes him. At the same time his
notions are precious and not invalidated. But for all his
absurdity he is Herzog for good or bad. "*I* am Herzog.
I have to *be* that man. There is no one else to do it. After
smiling, he must return to his own Self and see the thing
through."34 And properly to be that self he has to move
beyond ideas, temporarily at least, and re-establish
contact with ordinary reality.

This provides the ending of the book. Taking his
daughter out, he has a car crash. He has some exhausting, troublesome hours with the police because of the
revolver found on him. And this is where he really starts
to relax, to descend "from his strange, spiraling flight
of the last few days."35 He asks himself:

Is this, by chance, the reality you have been looking
for, Herzog, in your earnest Herzog way? Down in
the ranks with other people—ordinary life? By yourself you can't determine which reality is real?36

Bailed out by his brother he returns to his old country
house. Taking an inventory of its great disorder and
mess, he seems at the same time to be taking stock of
the mess of his own life. He feels a strange joy, relaxed
and liberated. Liberated, not only from Madeleine, but
from excessive exhausting egotism, the curse of unending
thought, the compulsive desire to explain everything
and legislate mentally for the whole world. Madeleine
said he was "sick with abstractions," and another
woman tells him his "ideas get in the way." He feels there
is some truth in this. He realises that perhaps he
has been making an error in "going after reality with
language."[37]

A new calm starts to grow in him because he gradually
ceases to strive for comprehension. "Go through what is
comprehensible and you conclude that only the in-
comprehensible gives any light."[38] He is sure that life is
more than "mere facticity." Faith grows in him, as he
starts to move beyond his verbalising, intellectualising,
self-preoccupation and self-importance. Quoting approvingly the Whitman line—"Escaped from the life that
exhibits itself"—he comes to a realisation of the dangers
of that narcissism which makes an individual set himself
up as a witness, an exemplar. He is learning a new
humility, reacquainting himself with the ordinary with
deep gladness. The curse is lifting and he is on the verge
of a new health, stirred by "indefinite music within."
Instead of worrying at the world with his theories he
relaxes, "feeling that he was easily contained by everything about him."[39] To calm his imagination, excited
by a new happiness, he paints a piano for his daughter.
At the same time "To God he jotted several lines":

> How my mind has struggled to make coherent sense. I have
> not been too good at it. But have desired to do your unknowable
> will, taking it and you, without symbols. Everything of
> intensest significance. Especially if divested of me.[40]

He decides to "lay off certain persistent torments. To surrender the hyperactivity of this hyperactive face. But just to put it out instead to the radiance of the sun."[41] He starts thinking about a more ordinary, sane future; instead of perverse self-communing—"*work. Real, relevant work.*"[42] "I mean to share with other human beings as far as possible and not destroy my remaining years in the same way. Herzog felt a deep, dizzy eagerness to *begin*."[43] The prose of this last chapter is extremely specific and at the same time brimming with lyricism. It communicates Herzog's new delight in the simple objects in his house, and the loveliness of the summer garden; his dawning reverence for the concrete, the rich plenitude of the seen world. At the same time it catches his inner, trembling fervour as he moves beyond thought to a mood which is almost mystical. He is surcharged with a strange joy—mortal, but with transcendent intimations. "*This strange organization, I know it will die. And inside—something, something, happiness. . . .*"[44]

The "spell" of the last few months is passing. "Perhaps he'd stop writing letters. Yes, that was what was coming, in fact. The knowledge that he was done with those letters."[45] The last scene of the book leaves Herzog, stretched out on a couch, for the first time experiencing a true pervading quiet after the remorseless inner clamouring which has racked him throughout the book. "At this time he had no messages for anyone. Nothing. Not a single word."[46] So the book ends. The resolution is completely internal. Externally there is still mess extending in all directions, but he has won through to a new attitude to it and seems at least able to re-enter it in a more tranquil spirit. His new good intentions are not shown in action; we do not see the common life he intends to lead nor do we see him sharing his life with other human beings. The book takes

Herzog to the end of his sickness and the promise of
cure. The inward work has been done. He has endured
thought and memory to the point of madness and
breakdown: now he is passing beyond them into a
mood of calm quiescent readiness. More genuinely
than in any previous book by Bellow, we feel a novel,
joyous sanity growing out of the neurotic exhaustion.
No new meanings, no solutions: rather a change of heart,
a turning to the sun. Not resignation but a profound
"let be," accompanied by peace and a prayer of praise
such as can only be uttered the other side of suffering.

REFERENCES

1. *H.*, p. 220.
2. *H.*, p. 2.
3. *H.*, pp. 272-3.
4. *H.*, p. 322.
5. *H.*, p. 34.
6. *H.*, p. 68.
7. *H.*, p. 72.
8. *H.*, p. 181.
9. *H.*, p. 278.
10. *H.*, p. 307.
11. *H.*, p. 265.
12. *H.*, p. 259.
13. *H.*, p. 181.
14. *H.*, p. 181.
15. *H.*, p. 144.
16. *H.*, p. 191.
17. *H.*, p. 125.
18. *H.*, p. 218.
19. *H.*, p. 162.
20. *H.*, p. 39.
21. *H.*, p. 160.
22. *H.*, p. 93.
23. *H.*, p. 129.
24. *H.*, p. 39.
25. *H.*, p. 125.
26. *H.*, p. 162.
27. *H.*, p. 49.
28. *H.*, p. 240.
29. *H.*, p. 316.
30. *H.*, p. 317.
31. *H.*, pp. 74-5.
32. *H.*, p. 125.
33. *H.*, p. 155.
34. *H.*, p. 67.
35. *H.*, p. 284.
36. *H.*, p. 287.
37. *H.*, p. 272.
38. *H.*, p. 266.
39. *H.*, p. 325.
40. *H.*, p. 236.
41. *H.*, p. 326.
42. *H.*, p. 314.
43. *H.*, p. 322.
44. *H.*, p. 340.
45. *H.*, p. 341.
46. *H.*, p. 341.

CHAPTER VIII

CONCLUSION: ISOLATION AND AFFIRMATION

In the midst of the continual movement that agitates a democratic community, the tie that unites one generation to another is relaxed or broken. . . . It is not only confidence in this or that man which is destroyed, but the disposition to trust the authority of any man whatsoever. Everyone shuts himself tightly within himself and insists upon judging the world from there.[1]

No Church, no State emerges; and when we have extricated ourselves from all the embarrassments of the social problem, the oracle does not yet emit any light on the mode of individual life. A thousand negatives it utters, clear and strong, on all sides; but the sacred affirmative it hides in the deepest abyss.[2]

These two quotations—the first from Tocqueville, the second from Emerson—written not so very far apart in time, offer a fitting introduction to a short concluding discussion of Bellow's work to date; for the problem of the unrelated self-enclosedness of the individual and the need for some "sacred affirmative" provide much of the motivating energy and material of his work. It has often been noted how lonely, insulated, and self-absorbed his main characters are. Where the novels are not actual first-person autobiography by the main character, they remain almost exclusively within a single consciousness. Joseph took refuge in his diary: Herzog writes letters which are never sent. There is not a great difference; solitary self-communing is really the main subject of Bellow's novels, as it is the habit and the disease of his heroes, or the sentence passed on them. It is of course a modern plight: "You had to talk with yourself in the daytime and reason with yourself at night. Who else was there to talk to in a city like New York?"[3] This is why there is so little action in his novels. His characters seem to be in a state which outside reality cannot really penetrate for any length of time. So hyperactive are their minds and memories that present life is never allowed to intrude for very long. Few of them actually *do* anything of much significance—a lot of Augie's adventures tend to be sexual in a not very profound way, while Henderson's puffings and blowings expend themselves in a land of romance. Bellow's characters want to understand the world, but they do not know how to act in it. As long as they are in a realistic setting they tend to be passive and immobile, neurotically lost in their own thoughts. They are as impotent and introspective as those lame, out-of-touch characters whose prevalence in modern literature Bellow lamented. Joseph is an underground man, and Herzog—so often prone and musing—is touched with Oblomovism. Not that they are complacent about this condition. Joseph yearns for some true community and Herzog really believes "that brotherhood is what makes a man human. . . . 'Man liveth not by Self alone but in his brother's face'. . . . The real and essential question is one of our employment by other human beings and their employment by us. Without this true employment you never dread death, you cultivate it."[4]

But in neither novel do we see the yearning and conviction put into practice. His characters want to establish relationships with other individuals and participate meaningfully in society but they do not know how to. Discussing Henderson, Norman Mailer made a point about Bellow which is valid for all Bellow's work: "he creates individuals and not relations between them, at least not yet."[5] Their relations with society bear out a general point made by Arthur Miller: "To think of an individual fulfilling his subjective needs through social action, to think of him as living most completely when he lives most socially, to think of him as doing this, not as a social worker acting out of conscientious motives, but naturally, without guilt or sense of oddness—this is difficult for us to imagine."[6] Although they want to enter society, their notion of social fulfilment is often theoretic and ideal. The inner world seems more real to them than the outer, public world—no matter how much they may lament the fact. It is not for nothing that the last book which Herzog dips into is by a Russian who asserts "that private life is above everything. . . . It is joy to be choked with thought."[7] Herzog has come to find it a curse and is willing to move out of the private realm. But—as with other Bellow figures—we never see this willingness made concrete in a new way of life. Consider the endings of the novels. A man capitulating to the army, another sobbing in a funeral parlour; Augie standing in the cold French countryside, Henderson running around the Arctic wastes between plane stops. Herzog we leave on a couch in a disordered house in the country. All have tasks and journeys unfinished, problems unsolved, resolutions untested. These endings are vivid pictures— momentary gestures of hope, readiness, and reconciliation: they are often vibrantly, emotionally "right"— but from another point of view they could also be called "conclusions in which nothing is concluded."

They yearn to commence a proper life, to participate in ordinary existence but, like Herzog, they never quite "reach the scene of the struggle."[8] We never see them emerge from the boundless and lonely confines

B—H

of their uninterrupted (and often uninterruptible) subjectivism. Georg Lukács has made some very pertinent comments on just this particular *malaise*. He maintains that it is "the opposition between a man and his environment that determines the development of his personality," and that much modern literature "by exalting man's subjectivity, at the expense of the objective reality of his environment" has in fact impoverished human life. He points to "the attenuation of actuality" in much modern literature and relates it to the "surrender to subjectivity" which is so prevalent in our age. What tends to happen is that we start to lose "the contours of individuality," and find it hard to gain a sense of "a man's actual fate" when the literary work focuses on a brooding interior consciousness. Since there is no proper action, no "dialectic between the individual's subjectivity and objective reality" we lose the sense of an actual realised man inhabiting a solid identifiable world. We may have a vast vague sense of man's "abstract potentiality": but character becomes blurred as though personality was disintegrating. The result is works which tend to be "static and sensational" rather than "dynamic and developmental."[9]

Now much of this can be applied to *Herzog*, where the main character is in some ways more of a presence than a person and where there is really very little *dialectic* between Moses and external reality (though there are plenty of bruising collisions and some embraces). There are some incomparable descriptions of external reality—from insects and trees to shops and traffic-jams—but somehow Moses does not seem to be truly related to it, even though at the end we do see him sinking down into "the lap of the actual" (Henry James), trying to slough off subjectivity. The remaining feeling is of a man somehow dislodged or left out of the continuum of the physical world—an unwilling refugee from reality banished to lasting inwardness. Of course, Bellow is aware of all this, the dangers and damages of subjectivism—indeed it is part of the distinction of his work to have explored those dangers so thoroughly and to have recognised the problem so fully. But the fact remains that he has yet to show the compulsive subjectivism of his characters actually transcended.

All this, I think, goes some way to explain the shortcomings in Bellow's work. Since his characters really don't do much his books lack the spine of a plot, they lack the impact of a sequence of linked incidents. They have no dramatic necessity. This means that there is a noticeable discrepancy between the tenor and the vehicle of Bellow's art. The internal emotional and intellectual development can be moving and convincing; the external chain of events which accompanies this change is often meagre, and unconvincing. Since Bellow equates—quite fallaciously to my mind—a concern for form with a contempt for ordinary life, he is left with very little to shape his work, for the passive character and the meandering speculating mind are the very reverse of organising forces. There is no necessary limit to reminiscence and metaphysical speculation, and Bellow's characters can abandon themselves to these for a long time without running into solid obstacles. Similarly with the style. Amazingly vivid and energetic, graphic in its descriptive force and dazzling in its expression of thoughts, it can also be profligate, uneconomical, and indiscriminate. It can be exhilerating in its cascading vitality, breathtaking in its robust assimilatory zeal, very humane in the attention it loves to lavish on the humblest particulars of ordinary life. It can be comic and woeful, physical or metaphysical— whatever the mood of the central character. But at times it seems to be straining too hard, trying to create by sheer richness and intensity of language beliefs and emotions which are not actually there. In Bellow's work, a great deal is talked about and thought about, but very little is enacted or actually experienced. His subject is the lone individual, passive and locked-up in himself, seeing things but not relating to them, talking to himself but not the world: whose reality is mainly composed of the words of his self-communing, whose action is the discontinuous movements of his own mind. Bellow's style can evoke all this with great authenticity.

In returning so often to the predicament of the isolated individual, Bellow is of course addressing himself to one of the deepest problems of our age. In an early book review of Gide he showed how aware he was of the theme which was to preoccupy him for so many of the coming years. He notes that Gide is "an excellent monologist who wants to advance to dialogue":

> The truth of monologue is exciting, but it is generally accidental in character; a man has only his own abilities to judge it with and the assistance of other men, if he is a confirmed monologist, does not easily become available to him . . . as human isolation increases while education and abilities multiply, the most vital questions and answers become the internal ones. Sadly enough, the number of intelligent people whose most vital conversation is with themselves is growing.[10]

Bellow knows that "dialogue, not monologue, is the foundation of a civilised life": but he also knows that "the life of a civilised man is, increasingly, an internalized one." His own work is full of "excellent monologists who want to advance to dialogue," but it cannot honestly be said that the advance has been made. What often happens is that, failing to experience any specific sense of relationship with other people and contemporary society, Bellow's characters respond to a more mystical sense of one-ness with some "larger body" which is transpersonal and relates them to the very currents of Being. Outcasts of society, they yet have moments when they feel at home in the universe. Tommy Wilhelm aches and weeps for all men who must die, but he is far from sorting things out with his wife and father. At the end of his exhausting introspective journey Herzog seems closer to some vague beneficient "God" than to the very human Ramona who is coming to dinner. Certainly, after this exalted communion he seems ready to re-enter common life in a simpler, humbler manner which may facilitate those human contacts he desires. But although the monologue has ceased, at least for the moment, the dialogue of civilisation has not yet begun. This is not Bellow's fault: the breakdown of that dialogue is a recognised phenomenon. A perceptive comment he made on current American novelists necessarily reflects on him as well. "American novelists are not ungenerous, far from it, but as their idea of society is fairly shallow, their moral indignation is non-specific. What seems to be lacking is a firm sense of a common world, a coherent community, a genuine purpose in life."[11] This is lacking in his own work. He has been drawn to the alienated, the neurotic, the suffering, the messed-up, those who run alone or wander and brood apart. Perhaps it is this experience of extremes that has lead him to assert the need for norms: "a firm sense of a common world, a coherent community, a genuine purpose in life." As he goes on to add, "No one can will these things into being and establish them by fiat." But you can search, as Bellow's characters have searched. And the fact that Herzog genuinely reaches a point where he seems on the point of acquiring that needed "firm sense" of reality and community—even if we have yet to see how it alters his daily life—seems to indicate that Bellow has completed a major phase in his evolution as a writer.

There is, nonetheless, a vein of paradox running through Bellow's characters which deserves more comment. They are alone and insulated, yet they stress the value of relationship; alienated and sometimes in flight from society, they still dream of true community. They would be free, but they want a shaping identity. They speak of their reverence for the indiscriminate stuff of life around them (and Bellow's style attests to the sincerity of this respect and love), yet their energy is often spent in disburdening themselves of hampering things; at times it seems as though they would like to disentangle themselves from matter altogether, and all the constricting feelings of limitation and determinism inherent in it. This syndrome does seem particularly American, thus Lionel Trilling can write:

From one point of view, no people has ever had so intense an idea of the relationship of spirit to its material circumstances as we in America now have. . . . it is to be seen that those conditions to which we do respond are the ones which we ourselves make, or over which we have control, which is to say conditions as they are virtually spirit, as they deny the idea of the conditioned. *Somewhere in our mental constitution is the demand for life as pure spirit.* It is this that explains the phenomenon of our growing disenchantment with the whole idea of the political life, the feeling that although we are willing, nay eager, to live in society, for we all piously know that man fulfills himself in society, yet we do not willingly consent to live in a particular society of the present, marked as it is bound to be by a particular economic system, by disorderly struggles for influence, by mere approximations and downright failures.[12] [My italics].

Bellow is clearly aware of all the paradoxes mentioned. They are important paradoxes, not to be solved, but to be deeply probed. It is the vigour and tenacity with which he explores these paradoxes that give Bellow his importance and centrality in contemporary literature.

It is not surprising that there is a general consensus among critics that Bellow is the most important of the post-war American novelist (although this book went to press before the critical reception of *Herzog* could be examined). In brief, the reasons are not far to seek. He is, perhaps, the most sheerly *intelligent* of post-war novelists, and although sections of his work tend to lapse into a sort of metaphysical garrulity, he is clearly well equipped to cope with the innumerable ideas which press upon the contemporary individual. Added to that, his ability to catch the texture of modern environment and the quality of his childhood world is incomparable. His prose often has the bulky vividness of heavy pigment—its power of vital evocation is remarkable. Then again his work shows a distinct progress: from a sulky, even churlish mood of passive non-participation, through a mood of celebration of the self, thence to a quest into the complex meaning of selfhood, on to a genuine attempt to affirm positive values which transcend the self altogether.

Much of Bellow's work—novels and articles— addresses itself to the problems, worth, and responsibility of modern "selfhood"; "the Self is losing its firm outline." In a talk on "Recent American Fiction," he discussed this point at length, making points which illuminate both the plight of his characters and himself as an author. He speaks of the contemporary American writer:

Laboring to maintain himself, or perhaps an idea of himself (not always a clear idea), he feels the pressure

of a vast public life, which may dwarf him as an individual while permitting him to be a giant in hatred
or fantasy. . . . Adapting Gresham's theorem to the
literary situation one might say that public life drives
private life into hiding. People begin to hoard
their spiritual valuables. Public turbulence is largely
coercive, not positive. It puts us into a passive position.
. . . Public life, vivid and formless turbulence, news,
slogans, mysterious crises, and unreal configurations
dissolve coherence in all but the most resistant minds
and even to such minds it is not always a confident
certainty that resistance can ever have a positive
outcome.

He sees that a major problem has become that of "the
single Self in the midst of the mass," and notes that
"the individual in American fiction often comes through
to us. . . . as a colonist who has been sent to a remote
place, some Alaska of the soul." Too many novels "are
filled with complaints over the misfortunes of the sover-
eign Self": Bellow dislikes all such egotistical moaning
and "unearned bitterness." He does not like those
writers who simply retire—defensively and despairingly
nourishing their own "sensibility." Nor does he like those
who take their battle against the old concept of the Self
too far. "Modern literature is not satisfied to dismiss a
romantic, outmoded conception of the Self. In a spirit
of deepest vengefulness it curses it. It hates it. It rends
it, annihilates it. . . . But after this destruction, what?"
This is a key point for Bellow's work. "I myself am not
convinced that there is less 'selfhood' in the modern
world. I am not sure anyone knows how to put the
matter properly." That is the problem eating into the
minds of his characters, who alternately over-estimate
and under-estimate the self, cursing or laughing at the
excesses of self-consciousness, yet refusing finally to
relinquish a sense of possible individual worth.

Undeniably the human being is not what he commonly thought a century ago. The question nevertheless remains. He is something. What is he? And this question, it seems to me, modern writers have answered poorly. They have told us, indignantly or nihilistically or comically, how great our error is but for the rest they have offered us thin fare.[13]

Bellow has himself tried most of the usual responses to the question, and he now clearly, urgently, wants to move on to some less denunciatory answer, which will hold out some hope neither ridiculous nor false. "I do not believe that human capacity to feel or do can really have dwindled or that the quality of humanity has degenerated." This has been his basic, inalienable contention. Agreed, the Self needs to be redefined; but he will not rest content with a pessimism which degrades human worth. Novelists "must value human existence or be unfaithful to their calling."[14] In the play he has just finished called *In the Last Analysis*, Bellow can be seen working feverishly—and comically—to get at some transcendent notion of a new selfhood which will take us out of our contemporary floundering among out-dated or sterile conceptions of ourselves. In it a famous, now slightly insane comedian, gives a last weird T.V. show in which he conducts a sort of Freudian inquiry down into the deepest roots of his self-history acting out every last little trauma. I have only seen a first draft, but among the comedian's remarks which accompanied some of the extremely funny scenes were these: "What we want now is the Upper Depths. Transcendence. . . . People who really live—who really die. Not this shuffling." "I'm not going to accomplish this. As though I were a saviour, I'm too grotesque. Still, I can aim my grotesqueness in a new direction. Maybe a new era will come." "My inner and outer life didn't match. Too vivid inside, too dead outside. Man has to express his condition—you hear me. Ex-press it. He can't be happy in an unreal state very long. He must know. Must! Must know. Truly! If he is sucked away from reality by the suction of civilization he will take a bloody revenge and annihilate everything." He is violent, hysterical, ecstatic as he tries to burst through into some new kind of Self. Like Herzog, he is tired of ideas and self-preoccupation, denouncing what he calls "this giant insanity of self-examination," in-sisting that "It's time the human mind began to be free from its own nonsense. Greater mysteries are waiting to be investigated." But again the paradox obtains: the play itself *is* a bout of insane self-examination. Perhaps it is therapy: a sloughing off of the old before the new can be born. But the new era is not ushered in, nor is the self visibly transcended. One is moved by the unleashed rhetoric of his vision and sense of need: at the same time one laughs at his mad antics. But we are not lead "from mere projections into the light of reality."

Still, Bellow will not rest content in a negative stance. Fiedler maintains that "to fulfill its essential moral obligation, [serious] fiction must be negative," and adds that for contemporary American novelists "the pursuit of the positive means stylistic suicide." They should say "No! in thunder."[15] Bellow has two points to make against that extreme position: "First, the idiocy of orthodox optimism ought not to provoke an equal and opposite reaction. Second, no one should found his nay upon the study of literature." He is, of course, not interested in didactic literature, but he feels that the morality of literature consists of the gesture towards life it makes:

either we want life to continue or we do not. If we don't want it to continue, why write books? . . . But

if we answer yes, we do want it to continue, we are
liable to be asked how. In what form shall life be
justified? That is the essence of the moral question.
We call a writer moral to the degree that his imagination indicates to us how we may answer naturally
without strained arguments, with a spontaneous
mysterious proof that has no need to argue with
despair.[16]

I think it can be argued that there is in fact a literature
of negative energy which is yet affirmative of life by the
vigour with which it excoriates false values, or in the
horror it awakens in us by revealing the waste, inade-
quacy, or cruelty of our lives. Then again, a writer may
find life terrifying or confusing and seek some solace
and staying power in the careful craft by which he
charts the terror and confusion. He may prefer to assert
the superior consolations of imagination over matter.
And I do not think Bellow would argue with this. His
own position is dignified, deeply sincere, never glib
or facile and, in our times, something of a necessity.
It is dangerous to become too domiciled in the abyss,
and a writer who can turn our eyes to the light above
does us a great service. Bellow is surely right in stressing
a current need for some new positive values. His own
work is most honest and compelling when it points to
that need. As we have seen, he cannot produce an
authentic image of the desiderated new way of life.
His work is full of would-be celebrants, moving slowly,
heavily, out of some over-long and suffocating imprison-
ment in their own consciousnesses.

Some critics find a positive affirmative joy, a mood
of radiant reconciliation in his work (one critic thinks
it is specifically Hassidic). I think there are a few such
moments, but Bellow does hit some false, too strident,
too assertive notes in this area. There is such a thing as

unearned gladness as well. What he does show is the movement towards such a joy, the dawning recognition that such a reconciliation should not be an impossibility. He shows us contemporary man in all the comedy and anguish of trying to cope with the disorderly mess of modern life pouring in from all sides, haunted by failure, threatened by insanity. He knows the "thousand negatives" that can be uttered about the individual life; he knows too that "the sacred affirmative" will not easily be found. But he believes it is and must be a possibility, and he is working to make sure that, should it be uttered, it will be understood. This is an honourable position, not without distinguished precedents. I quote some words from Conrad—not usually considered a facile optimist; words with which, I think, Bellow would concur.

I would require from him [the artist] many acts of faith of which the first would be the cherishing of an undying hope. . . . It is the God-sent form of trust in the magic force and inspiration belonging to the life of this earth. . . . What one feels so hopelessly barren in declared pessimism is just its arrogance. It seems as if the discovery made by many men at various times that there is so much evil in the world were a source of proud and unholy joy unto some of the modern writers. That frame of mind is not the proper one in which to approach seriously the art of fiction. It gives an author—goodness only knows why—an elated sense of his own superiority. . . . To be hopeful in an artistic sense it is not necessary to think that the world is good. It is enough to believe that there is no impossibility of its being made so.[17]

The last word with Bellow:

If the human pride of artists has indeed exhausted the miracle of this world then nothing in art is neces-

sary, all is superfluous. But here is the living man,
and the last word concerning him cannot be imagined.
We shall never know him in his entirety. Now, waiting
in darkness to be reanimated by a fresh impulse, we
feel painfully the weight of everything superfluous.
. . . But we know that something necessary, something
not to be evaded, is due and overdue.[18]

REFERENCES

1. A. de Tocqueville, *Democracy in America*, New York, 1959, Vol II, p. 4.
2. Emerson, *Works*, 1903, Vol. x, p. 218.
3. *S.T.D.*, p. 113.
4. *H.*, pp. 272-3.
5. "Norman Mailer versus Nine Writers," *Esquire*, IX, No. 1, Jul. 1963.
6. Arthur Miller, Introduction to *A View from the Bridge*, 1955, p. 6.
7. *H.*, p. 321.
8. *H.*, p. 128.
9. G. Lukács, *The Meaning of Contemporary Realism*, London, 1962, pp. 20-28.
10. "Gide as Writer and Autobiographer," 1951.
11. *The Great Ideas Today*, 1963, p. 177.
12. Lionel Trilling, *The Opposing Self*, London 1955, pp. 90-1.
13. "Recent American Fiction," One of the Gertrude Clarke Whittall Lectures, issued as a pamphlet by the Library of Congress. Also reprinted in *Encounter*, Nov. 1963.
14. *Twentieth Century Authors*, First Supplement, ed. Stanley Kunitz. 1955, pp. 72-3.
15. Leslie Fiedler, *No! In Thunder*, London 1963, p. 18.
16. "The Writer as Moralist," 1963.
17. J. Conrad, *Notes on Life and Letters*, London 1949, pp. 8-9.
18. From an unpublished typescript of a talk called "The Next Necessary Thing."

SELECT BIBLIOGRAPHY

The most comprehensive bibliography published to date was
compiled by Harold W. Schneider and appeared in *Critique*, III,
No. 3 (Summer 1960). My own select bibliography is heavily
indebted to Mr Schneider's, and his should be consulted by those
particularly interested.

I. SAUL BELLOW

1. *Novels*

Dangling Man. New York (Vanguard) 1944; London (John
    Lehmann) 1946.

The Victim. New York (Vanguard) 1947; London (John Lehmann)
    1948.

The Adventures of Augie March. New York (Viking Press) 1953;
    London (Weidenfeld and Nicolson) 1954.

Seize the Day. New York (Viking Press) 1956; London (Weidenfeld
    and Nicolson) 1957.

Henderson the Rain King. New York (Viking Press) 1959; London
    (Weidenfeld and Nicolson) 1959.

Herzog. New York (Viking Press) 1964; London (Weidenfeld and
    Nicolson) 1965.

2. *Short Stories*

The stories marked * appeared in the American edn. of *S.T.D.*
but not in the English edn.

"Two Morning Monologues," in *Partisan Review*, May-Jun. 1941.

"The Mexican General," in *Partisan Review*, May-Jun. 1942.

"A Sermon by Doctor Pep," in *Partisan Review*, May 1949.

"Trip to Galena," in *Partisan Review*, Nov.-Dec. 1950.

* "Looking for Mr. Green," in *Commentary*, Mar. 1951.

* "A Father-to-be," in *New Yorker*, 5 Feb. 1955.

* "The Gonzaga Manuscripts," in *Discovery*, No. 4, ed. V. Bourgaily.
    New York. (Pocket Books) 1956.

3. *Miscellaneous*

All reviews and articles of any importance are mentioned in the notes to the various chapters. The following is a selection.

"Dreiser and the Triumph of Art," in *Commentary*, May 1951.

"Gide as Writer and Autobiographer," in *New Leader*, 4 Jun. 1951.

"The Swamp of Prosperity," in *Commentary*, July 1959.

"The Uses of Adversity," in *Reporter*, 1 Oct. 1959.

"Address by Gooley MacDowell to the Hasbeens Club of Chicago," in *Hudson Review*, Summer 1951.

"Distractions of a Fiction Writer," in *The Living Novel*, ed. Granville Hicks. New York (Macmillan) 1957.

"Foreword" to Dostoevsky: *Winter Notes on Summer Impressions*. New York (Criterion Books) 1955.

"The Sealed Treasure," in *Times Library Supplement*, 1 Jul. 1960. Reprinted in *The Open Form*, ed. A. Kazin. New York (Harcourt Brace) 1961.

"A Talk with the Yellow Kid," in *Reporter*, 6 Sep. 1956.

Translation of I. B. Singer: "Gimpel the Fool," in *Partisan Review* May-June, 1953.

"The University as Villain," in *Nation*, 16 Nov. 1957.

"The Writer and the Audience," in *Perspectives USA*, Autumn 1954.

Introduction to *Great Jewish Short Stories*. New York (Dell) 1963.

"The Writer as Moralist," in *Atlantic Monthly*, March 1963.

"Recent American Fiction," in *Encounter*, November 1963.

"Literature," in *The Great Ideas Today*. New York (Encyclopaedia Britannica Inc.) 1963.

II. OTHERS

There are as yet no books on Saul Bellow. Two books contain long sections on his work, namely:

Eisinger, Chester: *Fiction of the Forties*. Chicago 1963.

Hassan, Ihab: *Radical Innocence—The Contemporary American Novel*. Princeton 1961.

Jack Ludwig's pamphlet, *Recent American Novelists*, Univ. of Minnesota Press 1962, has some pertinent comments on Bellow's work.

For biographical material, see *Twentieth Century Authors*, First
Supplement, ed. Stanley J. Kunitz. New York 1955.

The following is a selection of the most important critical articles
written on Bellow's work:

BRADBURY, MALCOLM: "Saul Bellow's *The Victim*," in *Critical
Quarterly*, Winter 1963.

CHASE, RICHARD: "The Adventures of Saul Bellow," in *Commentary*,
April 1959.

FIEDLER, LESLIE: "Saul Bellow," in *Prairie Schooner*, Summer 1957.

GEISMAR, MAXWELL: "Saul Bellow: Novelist of the Intellectuals,"
in *American Moderns: From Rebellion to Conformity*, New York
1958.

GOLD, HERBERT: "Fiction of the Fifties," in *Hudson Review*, Summer
1959.

GOLDBERG, GERALD: "Life's Customer, Augie March," in *Critique*,
Summer 1960.

JACOBSON, DAN: "The Solitariness of Saul Bellow," in *Spectator*,
22 May, 1959.

KAZIN, ALFRED: "The World of Saul Bellow," *The Griffin*, June
1959 (reprinted in *Contemporaries*, Boston 1962).

KLEIN, MARCUS: "A Discipline of Nobility," in *Kenyon Review*,
Spring 1962.

LEVENSON, J. C.: "Bellow's Dangling Men," in *Critique*, Summer
1960.

LEVINE, PAUL: "The Affirmation of the Philosophical Fool," in
Perspective, 10, Winter 1959.

WARREN, ROBERT PENN: "Man with no Commitments," in *New
Republic*, 2 Nov. 1953.

MALIN, IRVING: "Saul Bellow," in *London Magazine*, Jan. 1965.